COUNTERTOP
GARDENS

COUNTERTOP
GARDENS

Easily Grow Kitchen Edibles Indoors for Year-Round Enjoyment

SHELLEY LEVIS

COOL
SPRINGS
PRESS

Inspiring | Educating | Creating | Entertaining

Brimming with creative inspiration, how-to projects, and useful information to enrich your everyday life, Quarto Knows is a favorite destination for those pursuing their interests and passions. Visit our site and dig deeper with our books into your area of interest: Quarto Creates, Quarto Cooks, Quarto Homes, Quarto Lives, Quarto Drives, Quarto Explores, Quarto Gifts, or Quarto Kids.

First published in 2018 by Cool Springs Press, an imprint of The Quarto Group, 401 Second Avenue North, Suite 310, Minneapolis, MN 55401 USA. T (612) 344-8100 F (612) 344-8692 www.QuartoKnows.com

Cool Springs Press titles are also available at discount for retail, wholesale, promotional, and bulk purchase. For details, contact the Special Sales Manager by email at specialsales@quarto.com or by mail at The Quarto Group, Attn: Special Sales Manager, 401 Second Avenue North, Suite 310, Minneapolis, MN 55401 USA.

10 9 8 7 6 5 4 3 2 1

ISBN: 978-0-7603-5781-1

Library of Congress Cataloging-in-Publication Data

Names: Levis, Shelley, 1972- author.
Title: Countertop gardens : easily grow kitchen edibles indoors for
   year-round enjoyment / Shelley Levis.
Description: Minneapolis, MN : Cool Springs Press, 2018. | Includes index.
Identifiers: LCCN 2018003819 | ISBN 9780760357811 (sc)
Subjects: LCSH: Indoor gardening. | Plants, Edible.
Classification: LCC SB419 .L48 2018 | DDC 635/.2--dc23
LC record available at https://lccn.loc.gov/2018003819

Acquiring Editor: Todd Berger
Project Manager: Alyssa Lochner
Art Director: James Kegley
Cover Designer: Amy Sly
Layout: Amy Sly

On the front cover: Left, *courtesy of AeroGarden* by Miracle Gro; top right, *Shutterstock*; bottom right, *GAP Photos*

On the back cover: *Courtesy of Modern Sprout*

Printed in China

To Chris, for being my rock;
Rita and Leah, for keeping me grounded;
and Shawna, for planting the seed.

———————

TABLE OF CONTENTS

Introduction

Small space gardens and *indoor gardening* may be new catchphrases that have appeared in the last decade or so, but the methods are as old as dirt. The art of urban farming dates back many centuries, to when bustling cities like Paris in the 1670s needed to grow food year-round to feed its ever-growing population.

Innovative techniques using cold frames and the heat from decomposing horse manure extended the growing season and allowed more food to be grown in smaller areas. Fast forward to the square-foot gardening method, a technique Mel Bartholomew popularized back in the early 1980s, in which a small square area is divided into even smaller square growing sections. This, too, is not an entirely new concept, just an improved one. People grew parterres, or knot gardens, to produce herbs in organized beds in geometric patterns as early as the fifteenth century.

However, the term "small space gardening" is quickly becoming "no space" gardening, as many modern-day dwellings have little to no available outdoor areas to grow plants. Vertical gardening has become hugely popular as well, since growing *up* instead of *out* is the only option for some.

Luckily, innovations have come along that have greatly increased our access to fresh, home-grown food. Many books and publications written in just the last few years wouldn't have been able to discuss most of the devices mentioned in this book—the materials are that new.

Hydroponics, aquaponics, grow lights, and other high-tech equipment, once thought to be the tools of big commercial growers, are now available in scaled-down versions for homeowners. While there is a varying degree of required knowledge to operate such systems, there are plenty of systems available that can turn any brown thumb into a skilled gardener. The only digging required is to do research on which device will work best.

OPPOSITE A lot of food can be grown in a relatively small space.

Tumbler and cherry tomatoes are perfect for indoor growing.

The countertop devices available today might very well have put me out of a job. The innovative products designed for countertop gardening are changing how we grow and what we can grow indoors.

My path to countertop gardening started many years ago when I was in my mid-20s. I desperately wanted a garden in a small two-bedroom apartment that had a tiny balcony just big enough to fit a potted plant and folding metal chair. Desperation led to inspiration, and I began growing indoors. Since then, I have learned from my many failures: I've learned what methods lead to success and which plants are just simply better off grown outdoors. No amount of sweet talk is going to change that fact.

Back when I first started gardening indoors, the kinds of equipment and growing devices available today just didn't exist. Makeshift methods and barely tolerable décor adjustments were necessary if you were that bent on growing your own food indoors, as I was. Fortunately, my husband is extremely supportive of all my crazy ideas. His willingness to share office space with my grow operations of mesclun greens and lettuces was rewarded with many delicious meals.

As my passion for gardening grew, a desire to learn more led me to pursue a formal education in horticulture. I began my own business as a garden designer and took on jobs that centered around specialty and small space garden design.

Several of my clients were chefs seeking epicurean gardens at both their private residences as well as their restaurants. Growing methods had to accommodate ease of use in very limited space and provide fresh herbs, salad greens, and unique ingredients that were not readily available.

The countertop devices available today might very well have put me out of a job. The innovative products designed for countertop gardening are changing how we grow and what we can grow indoors. These devices allow professional chefs and foodies alike to grow ingredients right at their fingertips with very little gardening experience.

After several years of designing gardens, I felt it was time to share my experiences, and the blog "Sow & Dipity" was born. In addition to my writing, I currently hold a position as a retail garden center manager.

It should be no surprise that I oversee several departments, including seeding, edibles, and indoor gardening. The advantage of working in a garden center is that I get to keep a pulse on the latest products and interact with consumers seeking specific advice on their indoor growing needs.

In that environment, where things grow from floor to ceiling and you're constantly surrounded by organic bliss, no judgment takes place when you first meet someone. I know people by what they grow, not by what they do. Novices are treated like new recruits to the club, and sages are admired for their wisdom. I've had conversations about tomatoes with bearded bikers and shared lavender recipes with a police officer. No matter what a person does in their other life, we have something in common the moment they walk in the door.

Many of our discussions relate to growing indoors and having to deal with a lack of space. Add to this people's busy schedules and their desire for simplicity, and growing solutions need to fit their budgets and lifestyles.

These days, the sheer busy nature of my life—the speaking and writing and other demands—has overtaken the actual activity of gardening itself. And for this reason, having small manageable "grows" has become important to me, as well. With several small indoor spots of countertop greenery,

Specialty foods like heirloom carrots are not expensive when you grow them yourself. *Shutterstock*

I can still get my garden fix on these days when I'm necessarily focused on building my personal brand. My guess is that there are many of you out there who would like to do the same. And that's the reason for the book you are now reading.

Growing your own food isn't easy—if you're after simple, you go to a grocery store. But gardening fulfills more than just our stomachs. It is our birthright to feed ourselves with the effort of our own hands. Personally, I think such a skill is far more important than a dozen or so useless things we learn in school. Shouldn't growing and cultivating our own food be a mandatory subject? Why isn't the very act of self-sustainability not included in our schools' curriculums?

There has been a huge upsurge in elementary school gardens, and thankfully, there are a lot of modern-day pioneers paving the way to making this as common a class as chemistry. Planting the seeds early in young minds is the key to creating passionate stewards of our planet for the future.

Fancy foods such as purple carrots or fresh radish sprouts aren't intended to be just the epicurean delights of the wealthy, despite their costs at high-end restaurants and in grocery stores. The truth is, you can become a gourmand of rare vegetables and tender delicacies without all the expense. You just need to grow them yourself.

When I speak at big garden events like the Northwest Flower and Garden Show in Seattle, I take advantage of my time to step up onto my soapbox and deliver my message. I created my blog to inspire others to get growing. But I also think it's my duty to inspire others to also inspire others to get growing. This is an infection that, once you contract it, leads to green thumbs and dirt mustaches—and it is a very pleasant infection to have.

My hope is that this book inspires you to get growing too. All that is required is a countertop and a desire to grow fresh food. Over the coming pages, I'll cover the basics of plant care, suggest several varieties (not just types, but actual named varieties) of vegetables you can grow indoors, and share the many experiences I've had along the way, having been in this industry for more than 20 years now.

Every countertop growing device discussed in this book was personally tested by me and is currently, as I write these words, growing food. I have included DIY projects that you can do yourself with little effort and time, and fairly simple materials. Later, I share some troubleshooting tips and some great resources to help you and your countertop garden grow.

Regardless of where you are in your gardening journey, there is always something new to learn and that is what makes this hobby/passion so exciting. It's not a job you get done, it's an ever-changing opportunity to create.

When it comes to gardening, think outside the pot!

Self-contained indoor growing systems are becoming more efficient and more affordable with every passing year. *Photo by Shelley Levis*

Inspiration Gallery

Photos courtesy of Modern Sprout

ABOVE *Photo courtesy of Back to the Roots* OPPOSITE TOP *Photo courtesy of Modern Sprout*
OPPOSITE BOTTOM *Photo courtesy of SunBlaster*

ABOVE *Photo courtesy of Back to the Roots* OPPOSITE TOP *Photo courtesy of Modern Sprout*
OPPOSITE BOTTOM *Photo courtesy of Potting Shed Creations*

COUNTERTOP GARDEN METHODS

"How does your garden grow?"

The original writer of this line from an old nursery rhyme dating back as far as the eighteenth century certainly could never have imagined how food would be grown today. And surely they would be surprised at how food gardening is moving indoors onto countertops.

Practicing traditional gardening methods governed by seasons, geography, and even superstition has been how our species has survived since we pushed our first digging tool into the earth. Wives' tales and folklore peppered farmers' teachings as they passed their knowledge down to their offspring—generation after generation repeating the same steps taught to them, and always praying for good weather.

The term *husbandry* refers to how farmers care for their animals, their crops, and their land. Over time, systems became more advanced and the art of growing crops soon became the science of it. While some might say that the modern farm is too automated and that it bears little resemblance to the ways of our ancestors, I would argue that the high demand of feeding a growing population seeking fast, cheap food has left the farming industry with few choices.

It's easy to beat the "organic only" drum with little thought to how our food must be mass produced. As cities swell and farmland shrinks, doing more with less has become a necessity. Hence, non-organic, GMO,

A few of the devices I discuss in this book, in various stages of growth. From left to right: two AeroGardens, the Hydrofarm Salad Box, and the SunBlaster Micro Grow Light Garden and their full-size Grow Light Garden.

and chemically treated food was born. Food must travel long distances and last for extended periods of time. This requires the manipulating of the DNA traits of the meat and vegetables we consume, and thus changing genetic traits has become more important than preserving them.

Much of the food that lines our grocery store shelves is not really "real" food at all. Rather, these products probably are best considered "food-like" substances packed with just the right amount of sugar and fat to fool our brains into thinking we are eating something satisfying. As the

structure of family units changed and mothers took up careers to form two-earner households, convenience was king and the preference for grab-and-go food was born. Our society changed and so did our food.

But despite all the necessary convenience the modern-day grocery store has to offer us, another change is now forcing the pendulum to swing the other way. After a generation of consumers for whom growing their own food wasn't practical or appealing, the newest generation shows a true fascination again. Gardening is once again becoming not just a hobby for our grandmothers, but a growing trend infecting future green thumbs.

Working in a garden center, I'm blown away and inspired when I see young couples in their mid-20s shopping for seeds and supplies. While they show me pictures on their phones and ask me their many gardening questions, I remind myself that not only are they our future customers, they are also a massive consumer demographic with the power to influence agricultural practices in the years ahead.

What Is a Bedding Pack?

Exactly. For the last three years, I've been downsizing the flowering 606 pack section in our garden center's annual plants area. The generation that actually remembers what a bedding pack is finds itself also downsizing. The once popular bedding plant pack is being replaced by the instant color gratification of the 4-inch pot.

Space is at a premium for many new homeowners today, and having large swaths of flower beds bulging with blooms is not realistic. Open space on home lots is shrinking—partly because the lots themselves are shrinking and partly because the trend is to build ever larger houses within the footprint of the property site. And as open space is shrinking, so too is the time homeowners have available keep those beds looking great

At one time, most folks bought bedding packs in bulk, six-packs of six plants in a flat, to mass plant in their garden beds. But gardeners today are growing differently. For example, with limited room to grow wide, they are instead growing up, using vertical units designed for patio railings or skinny walls. And with less space—or even no garden bed at all for growing outdoors—gardeners are increasingly growing indoors with the help of devices specifically designed to produce fresh organic food right there on their countertops.

Those devices and their use are the subjects of this book. In an effort to share the many types of units available for countertop gardening, I spent time researching and acquiring these products to test-drive them before sharing my experiences with you.

Currently, there are about two dozen different types of indoor gardening devices growing plants on every available countertop, window ledge, and shelf in my home. Keeping all these growing devices operating on a daily basis has become a chore in itself, with lights clicking on and off, water pumps kicking in with an uprush of gurgles, and the constant monitoring for fungus gnats. Although my husband accepts the excuse that all this is "for the book," deep down he likely realizes that this new addiction will eventually require an intervention if he is ever to reclaim his office space.

Before we discuss the many different methods available for countertop gardening, we need to put down some roots and start from the ground up.

Growing Mediums

By *growing medium*, we're referring to the substrate, the material that plants are grown in. The main functions of a growing medium are:

- **To provide a place for roots to grow**

- **To supply nutrients, air, and water**

- **To provide physical support for the plants**

Selecting the growing medium that works best for your needs depends solely on how the plants will be grown. Container and hydroponically grown plants have different requirements than plants grown outdoors in garden beds. Potting mix sold in bags is a recipe that blends many different ingredients designed specifically for a purpose. For

THE DIRT ON DIRT

Garden soil is heavy and can contain a plethora of weed seeds, pests, and diseases. Although it may contain the nutrients a plant requires, poor drainage or too much of one element—such as clay or sand—could affect the plant's performance.

Garden soil that has been amended with compost or manure is ideal for most vegetable growing outdoors, but it's not suitable for plants in pots, since the amendments are usually still in a process of breaking down and not available for the immediate feeding requirements of fast-growing container-bound plants.

Perlite and vermiculite are the basis for many soilless mixes.

example, cactus soil will contain more sand and perlite for better drainage, while a container mix will have more peat for improved moisture retention. Many of these mixes are considered soilless, since they don't contain any actual "traditional" soil at all.

SOILLESS MEDIUMS

Soilless mixes used for container gardening and houseplants are considered sterile and free of contaminants. Producers of bagged potting mixes use some of the following ingredients in combination to create their recipes:

- **PEAT MOSS:** Consists of decomposed organic materials grown in peat bogs. It's lightweight, sterile, and has a good water-holding capacity.

- **PERLITE:** White in color, this is a form of expanded volcanic rock. It is key in providing good drainage, as it holds air and does not retain water.

- **VERMICULITE:** Often used as an alternative to perlite, this is a form of mica, but it does retain water. It does not provide the same aeration benefits that perlite does.

- **BARK AND WOOD MULCH:** Not suited for container planting, since mulch is high in carbon and lacks nutrients. However, it does aid in soil structure when added to garden soil.

- **SAND:** Increases drainage and adds air to a soil mix. Ideal for plants that prefer drier growing conditions.

- **COCONUT COIR:** Made from coconut husks, this renewable organic resource is lightweight, traps air, and retains water.

Various other nutrients in the form of slow-release fertilizers are often added to bagged potting soils. Pro-Mix soils have begun to use mycorrhizae in their soilless mixes over the last few years. The beneficial fungus can be found in undisturbed forests and lives symbiotically with plants and trees by colonizing their root systems. The fungi benefit from the plant's production of carbohydrates, while they also return the favor by delivering increased nutrient and water absorption back to the plant. This is Mother Nature's system of shaking hands between the microbes of the earth and the green giants that provide us with oxygen.

HYDROPONIC MEDIUMS

Hydroponics—the process of growing plants in a soilless medium in which nutrients are dissolved in water—may also use peat, sand, or coconut coir, but this method of growing has its own set of mediums in which plants are grown.

- **ROCKWOOL:** Most commonly used in hydroponics, this sterile, porous medium is made from granite or limestone broken down into small threads and formed into blocks, cubes, or sheets. It is highly absorbent and can actually suffocate plant roots if not used carefully. Rinsing—a lot of rinsing—is required in a pH-balanced water solution before using rockwool as medium.

- **OASIS:** This foam is used mainly by florists in their arrangements, and is highly absorbent as well. It has an open cell structure that gives roots plenty of room to grow.

Growing hydroponically requires specialty growing mediums and supplies.

- GROWSTONES: Made of a recycled glass aggregate that is lightweight, porous, and reusable, growstones are shaped like uneven pebbles. They have an amazing wicking ability and can draw water up above the water line.

- HYDROCORN: Lightweight expanded clay aggregate (LECA) is made from clay and is one of the most popular mediums used in hydroponics. This sterile growing medium is lightweight, holds moisture, wicks water to roots, and has a neutral pH. The round shape of the pebbles supports plants well in containers.

There are plenty of other products that are used to grow hydroponically, including rice hulls and water-absorbing crystals, but the four outlined above are the most common and best suited for beginners who are just diving in to water-based solution growing.

Growing in Soilless Mix

Making soil is actually "a thing." Or more accurately, it's not soil we're making, but a soilless mix.

My method was to spread a massive tarp out in my garage and make soil with my own special recipe, which included a large bale of peat, a big bag of perlite, several wheelbarrows of compost, and other nutrient additives, including a slow-release fertilizer. The batch was watered, then turned with a shovel, scooped into a giant pyramid in the center of the tarp, then pulled back out to the edges again with a garden fork.

This scooping and pulling was repeated several times, and I watered the batch each time it was laid out flat and used the back of my digging tools to break up the clods. After it was sufficiently mixed and moistened, I shoveled it into six large garbage cans and lined them up by my potting bench for use during the spring season.

"Hydrocorn" is a growing substrate made from formed and filed clay. It is used mostly in hydroponics.

This container potting mix was my own recipe for making hanging baskets and containers for my clients when I had my own garden design business many years ago. It wasn't light work, and the fluffy particles of peat had an amazing way of working themselves into my clothing. Taking off my socks and gloves revealed the lines of my "dirt tan," and my skin itched from the caked peat stuck to sweaty skin.

Luckily, commercially made mixes don't require this kind of effort. Choosing a good-quality potting soil for indoor growing is as easy as grabbing a bag off a shelf. Be sure to use one that specifies that it is organic, since the whole purpose of growing your own food is to avoid unwanted chemicals in the first place.

Growing Hydroponically

For my hydroponic projects, I have tested hydrocorn, rockwool, coir pellets, and growstones. I have gotten good results from all of them except the rockwool.

The reasons for my failure with rockwool are not entirely clear. Although I did rinse the cubes for hours with repeated rinses of fresh water and used a pH adjustment powder in the last few turns, the seedlings still did not "take." My intent was to transfer the rockwool cubes and seedlings to a container surrounded by hydrocorn once the second set of leaves developed, but they never made it that far.

Finding the rockwool process finicky, I chose instead to start the seedlings in coir pellets— flat disks of compressed coir similar to peat pellets. Once you add water, the disks swell to about six times their original size, forming little cylinder-shaped pods encased by a fine mesh fabric. Drop at least two to three seeds into the preformed hole on top and gently squeeze the pellet to cover them with the peat or coir.

Roots can easily push through the fine mesh as they grow, and once seedlings are established, the entire ball can then be transferred to a container with potting mix or used in a hydroponic system. The soil inside will not spill out, and the root ball is easy to handle. You will need to thin each pellet down to one seedling per root ball. There isn't

Peat or coir pellets are used for seed starting. They are easy to use and provide support for young seedlings.

enough room in these little pods to keep multiple seedlings healthy, so all but one of them must go.

Caring for pellets is easy while the young seedling is growing. Add water to the tray a little at a time, and the pellets will absorb what they need. You don't want them to become saturated, but you also don't want them to completely dry out, either. I put these pellets under a grow light while the plants develop and when they are ready, they move on to a hydroponic system to continue growing.

Seedling grown in a peat pellet.

Growing Aquaponically

This is a whole different kettle of fish, literally. Aquaponics can be complex systems in which you are growing not only plants, but fish as well. There is a third player in this cycle that has to be present in order for this method to work, and that is bacteria.

Mother Nature conducts aquaponics without any effort in ponds and streams. In a controlled, closed environment, however, it will require some skill and know-how.

This system of turning fish waste into food with the help of bacteria is all about balance. The

ammonia from the fish waste is not in a form that plants can use. It must first be converted into nitrates in the form of nitrogen. Microbes nitrify the bacteria that grows on the roots and surrounding substrate of plants; their job is to do this conversion. The plants then take up the nutrients produced by the microbes, which in turn purify the water being circulated back down to the fish.

Advanced aquaponics systems can be quite large, and gardeners who grow plants using this method may require a sizable backyard setup. Food fish can be raised in these grow beds and are also harvested for consumption. Fish stocking is dependent on your

Aquaponic

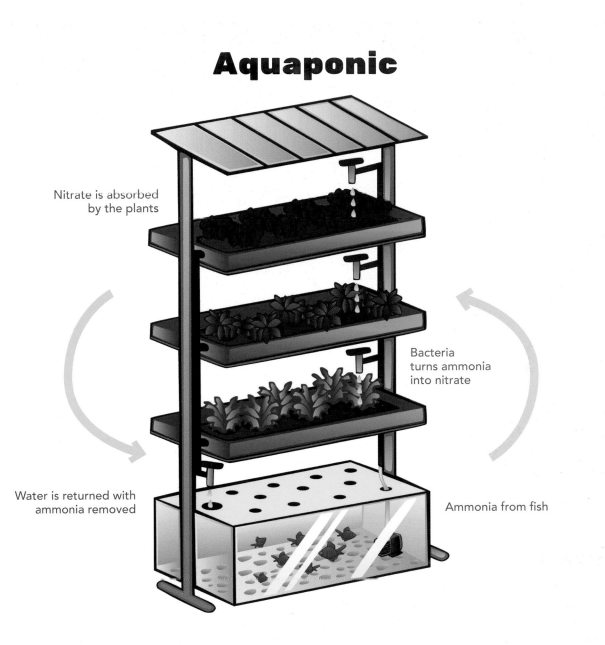

Nitrate is absorbed by the plants

Bacteria turns ammonia into nitrate

Water is returned with ammonia removed

Ammonia from fish

climate and geographical location. Cooler climates may grow trout, while warmer ones may grow tilapia. The fish don't necessarily need to be grown for eating—koi or goldfish could be raised and treated as family pets rather than dinner.

Since the purpose of this book is to concentrate on countertop gardening methods, we won't go into the specifics of a large-scale aquaponic system. However, it is possible to have a small system that will fit nicely next to a coffee pot or under a kitchen counter. I discuss one of these devices in the next chapter.

BARE ROOT METHOD

By far, this method will net you the quickest results when growing hydroponically. Buying lettuce and kale in six-packs or fiber packs is easy, since the seed starting part has already been done for you. Gently break apart the seedlings and run them under a hose with a watering wand set on a gentle spray to remove the excess soil.

Once the roots are free of the mix, they should be quickly moved to the hydroponic system to avoid drying out. Set them into net pots and use either hydrocorn or growstones to support them. For the first week, I constantly mist them as well, since the leaves will become quickly dehydrated. Don't worry too much if some of the outer leaves wither and die. As long as the center looks to be holding up, the plant should soon recover.

Seeds vs. Transplants

Obviously, starting from seed has its challenges, but the personal satisfaction of knowing you are the creator of your food right from the beginning is rewarding too. Growing from transplants increases your odds of success, and you'll be enjoying them on your dinner plate much sooner. Each method has its own pros and cons.

Use a gentle spray to remove as much soil from the roots as you can prior to planting in a hydroponic unit.
Photo by Shelley Levis

Starting from seeds gives you virtually unlimited options; unlike when you buy seedlings, you are not dependent on any nursery's growing schedule.

ADVANTAGES TO GROWING FROM SEEDS:

- Huge selection of what you want to grow, since you choose the seeds.

- More control over organic production through your choice of fertilizing.

- Cost is greatly reduced—one packet of forty seeds vs. one six-pack of transplants.

- Available to grow any time of year, regardless of season.

DISADVANTAGES TO GROWING FROM SEEDS:

- Greater risk of plant failure at early stages.

- Longer wait for production time.

- Requires special attention when first sown.

When direct-planting in growing mediums, sprinkle small seeds (such as lettuce) on the surface and dust a thin layer of soil over the top of them.

ADVANTAGES TO GROWING FROM TRANSPLANTS:

- Easy to grow larger plants.

- Ready for consumption in just a few weeks.

- Not as delicate when it comes care and watering.

DISADVANTAGES TO GROWING FROM TRANSPLANTS:

- Limited selection.

- Cannot guarantee 100 percent organically grown (from seed or feed).

- Vastly higher costs than for seeds.

- Not available throughout the year.

I recommend a combination of both seeds and transplants during the times of the year when transplants are available. In my home, there are plenty of trays of plants started from seed, all growing at different stages. But growing transplants in spring allows me to get faster results from healthy plants during a time of year when I'm craving lots of salads.

Succession cropping allows you to have a continuous supply of greens. Harvesting plants that are ready for eating while a new batch is coming up behind them just makes sense. At the garden center, people tell me that they have no luck with cilantro—that it just doesn't last. The truth is that cilantro just isn't one of those crops that continues on and on as you harvest it; you have to plant successive crops if you want to continue enjoying cilantro through the season.

Unlike other herbs or greens that can be harvested by the cut-and-come-again method, cilantro will eventually just become a mound of leafless green stems. Have a backup plan if you are one of those people who loves this herb and will be eating a lot of it. For example, you can drop seeds in with the cilantro transplants, and as they grow and are harvested, continue seeding in this manner. The same method works for several types of herbs and greens, such as arugula and cress.

Whatever way you wish to start growing is completely a personal choice. Some of the available devices, which we will discuss in the next chapter, provide planting pods or seeds designed for that specific unit, so this can be viewed as either limiting or freeing, depending on how you like to grow.

Most larger seeds, such as kale, do need to be buried in the soil, but not too deep. Usually two times the seed circumference is enough.

GROWING BASICS

Gardening can be intimidating when you're just starting out. Don't be afraid to ask questions. We all have to start somewhere, and gardening is not something you learn once—it is an ongoing lifelong learning adventure. This is just as true for those in the garden center profession as those who shop there.

I have to refer constantly to internet searches to look up new plant introductions. Each week dozens of availability sheets are sent in from our local growers to place orders, and there are always plant varieties that are new to me. It is impossible to know them all and to stay on top of individual care or unique problems that may plague them—and if this is true for someone who has been in the industry for close to twenty years, it is even more true for most home gardeners.

While there is plenty of information on the internet and in various books on the topic of indoor gardening and specific plants, the goal of this book is to deliver simple and practical advice that anyone, regardless of skill level, can use.

This chapter will focus on the basics of lighting, feeding, watering, and general care required for countertop gardening methods. The goal here is to green up those thumbs and get you started. Once you have the basics down and a few successes under your belt, you'll be ready to learn more and advance your skills to a higher level. The best way to learn is to just start, so let's dig in and get growing.

Photo courtesy of Modern Sprout

Let There Be Light!

Sunlight (or a viable substitute for real sunlight) is vital for all plants—and for all life on this planet, for that matter. It seems simple enough: put a plant near a window where there's light, and it will grow. Lighting is not a simple topic. Experts with years of experience in greenhouse growing and a list of degrees under their belts are constantly tweaking with artificial light sources to maximize growth rates.

Without getting too technical, let's examine the role light plays in plant growth and explore what forms of light are the most beneficial for our indoor growing needs.

The importance of light cannot be stressed enough, since it is absolutely essential for kick-starting the photosynthesis cycle. To simply say that plants basically just "eat sunlight" is to grossly oversimplify this incredible process. However, a full explanation is so complex that entire books are dedicated to this subject alone, so we'll have to settle for this basic metaphor for the process.

Light itself can be measured in several different ways. *Quantity*, *quality*, and *duration* are all significant factors. The quality of light is also dependent on the time of year, time of day, geographical location, and weather—all factors that can be controlled in an indoor growing situation.

- QUANTITY: **Different plants require light at different energy levels to start the process of photosynthesis.**

- QUALITY: **Color or wavelength of light is divided into three regions: ultraviolet, visible light (what humans see), and infrared. Different colors of light have different effects on plants.**

- DURATION: **Known as the photoperiod, this term refers to the number of hours of daylight per day.**

Grow lights come in several shapes and sizes, including fluorescent tube bulb and compact fluorescents, as well as several non-fluorescent types. *Photo by Shelley Levis*

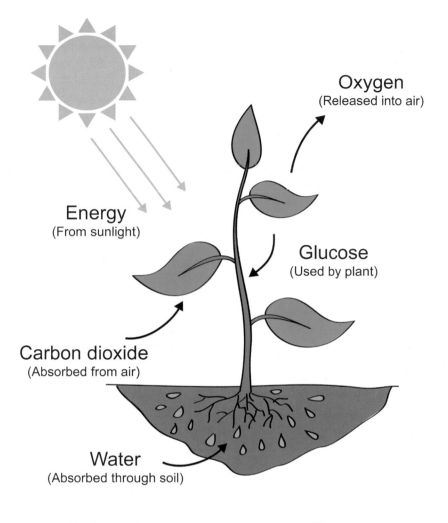

Oxygen
(Released into air)

Energy
(From sunlight)

Glucose
(Used by plant)

Carbon dioxide
(Absorbed from air)

Water
(Absorbed through soil)

Photosynthesis 101

The process of photosynthesis is how plants make their own food, and it is done in two steps. The first step involves a reaction dependent on light, and the second step involves a dark (light-independent) reaction.

A chemical process uses light energy absorbed by chloroplasts in plants' leaves to create a series of chain reactions. This produces molecules that convert and store this energy in the form of adenosine triphosphate (ATP)—an organic compound required for metabolic processes. The ATP that is stored drives another series of complex reactions known as the Calvin cycle. Carbon dioxide taken in by plants' foliage through air and water pulled up through the roots uses ATP to produce glucose and oxygen in the light-independent reaction. Both are equally necessary for this vital conversion of carbon dioxide, water, and light energy into glucose and oxygen. It's that simple.

Ultraviolet light can reduce the rate of photo-synthesis and cause DNA damage to the plant. Blue light is required for plants to produce vegetative and leaf growth; it is important that young plants receive enough blue light to prevent stretching. Red light is also vital, as it aids in flowering and fruiting. Far red light can create problems in plants by causing them to elongate when they receive a higher-than-normal ratio of far red light. We can see this in practice when seedlings and young plants located in a space that's too shaded begin to reach for the sun and become "leggy."

Different light sources deliver different types of light, often referred to as the light "temperature." This is not a literal measure of its actual temperature, but a subjective one. We understand this effect when we compare an office building that has fluorescent lighting versus a home space where incandescent bulbs are the norm. The color of light has a temperature associated with it: it can feel warm (more red) or cool (more blue). A combination of red and blue light is what is required for most plants to grow successfully.

Photoperiod refers to the length of time that plants receive light. Darkness plays a huge role in how and when plants flower, which is especially important for blooming types of plants. Photoperiod isn't measured necessarily by how much light plants receive, but rather by the opposite—by how much darkness they receive. To understand this, plants are divided into three photoperiod categories:

- **SHORT-DAY PLANTS: In spring and fall when nights are longer, short-day plants will form their flowers only when day length is less than 12 hours. Green onions, some strawberry varieties, sweet potatoes, and soybeans are examples of short-day vegetables.**

- **LONG-DAY PLANTS: In summer when nights are shorter and there are more hours of daylight, long-day plants will flower. Potatoes, carrots, beets, and peas fit in this category. Lettuce is also considered a long-day plant since it bolts to flower when exposed to days with long light.**

- **DAY-NEUTRAL PLANTS: These are plants that will set flowers regardless of day length and that are more reactive to seasonal temperatures. Tomatoes, peppers, corn, and cucumbers are good examples of this group.**

Evidence of how important light and darkness is to plants can be seen in the use of mums in seasonal gardening.

In my time managing garden centers, I have worked in several types of greenhouse operations and have learned how important light is in the mass production of plants. Sophisticated systems allow the control of light to be a very exact science, a science that allows us to force plants into bloom anytime of the year, regardless of the weather outside.

Timing was essential in order to push plants into stores exactly when they required them. Fall mums were among their main crops—approximately 200,000 cuttings were imported from other parts of the globe and were then grown in different bays, where lighting was controlled by the minute. Shipping began the first week of August and continued for two months into the fall. In order to hit the required ship dates, a computer-automated system was installed that was able to draw black-out cloth across the ceilings of different bays during the late spring and summer months, effectively fooling the plants into putting on buds at different stages. Timed perfectly, a new crop cracked color each week and was stuffed into trucks for delivery. Other mums were set out into the outdoor fields to continue growing, allowing them to color up according to Mother Nature's schedule.

In commercial greenhouses, the amount of light provided to the plants is critical to manipulating their environment to follow their natural growing patterns. For example, light is controlled to trick poinsettias into peaking at just the right time. You can do the same thing with plants in your home.

Some customers purchasing these mums that were forced into a timed bloom would later attempt to plant them in the garden, hoping for them to come back the next year. Sometimes they got lucky and the plant survived despite the fact that mums ride the line of hardiness in our zone. For others, though, mums that successfully overwintered and appeared lush and healthy would still refuse to set buds.

I always asked these folks to describe where this mum was planted. Was there a street lamp or house light interfering with its required photoperiod of darkness? Yes, this is how sensitive plants can be to light. A motion-activated light on a garage could be the culprit robbing you of fall color. A plant may simply be confused, with its internal clock believing that summer is not yet over.

Green onions are short-day plants and need longer cool nights to set buds. *Shutterstock*

The moral? Understanding the importance of light will aid you in growing successfully.

A variety of light sources for the home gardener are readily available today. Specialty grow lights formerly used exclusively by the horticulture industry and mass-production greenhouses have been shrunk down for use in the smallest of countertop growing devices.

Most of these countertop lights are designed to mimic natural daylight, providing precisely the right kind of light most plants require for optimal growth and offering ease of use right out of the package. Understanding lumens and Kelvin and all the other jargon that goes with grow lights can be overwhelming, but certainly there are plenty of resources out there if you wish to dive in deeper on this subject.

For the purpose of hobby gardening, visit a local retailer who sells products related to seed starting and growing, and you will most likely find the right light for your needs.

Fertilizer

Visiting the fertilizer department at a garden center is overwhelming even to the seasoned gardener. The shelves are stocked with hundreds of bottles, bags, and containers, all promising miraculous growth. How do you choose the right one for your needs?

Fortunately, most short-term leafy plants intended for consumption do not require a long-term feeding program. Fast-growing food plants are generally eaten within a short window, since they produce fruit or leaves during just a few months of the growing season. (Fruit-bearing trees are in a different category, of course, and are not included in this discussion of countertop gardening.)

When it comes to growing indoors, the goal is to create an environment as close to Mother

Selecting the best fertilizers for your countertop garden depends on many variables, including the plant species. To avoid being overwhelmed by the product selection at your local nursery, first do some homework on the needs of the specific plants you are growing.

Knowing your NPKs

Fertilizers all list a three-digit number on their packaging, indicating how much of each of the three primary nutrients plants need (nitrogen-phosphorus-potassium) can be found in that fertilizer.

This basic formula—NPK, standing for nitrogen, phosphorus, and potassium, respectively—represents the three primary nutrients required by every plant, tree, and shrub. The proportions of each nutrient varies, however, according to the needs of individual plants. When shopping for fertilizer, these are the three most obvious numbers visually represented on the package. In a fertilizer package labeled "10-20-10," for example, the numbers represent the percentages of nitrogen, phosphorus, and potassium, in that order.

- **N- NITROGEN:** This is essential for shoot growth in the form of leaves and green growth. Nitrogen helps plants produce chlorophyll for tissue development. Fertilizers intended to nourish lawn grasses have a high first number (nitrogen) content to assist in lush green growth.

- **P- PHOSPHORUS:** Phosphorus is needed for root and fruit growth. It aids in the metabolic process of transferring energy from one part of the plant to another. Fruit-bearing plants like tomatoes require phosphorus to set the flowers that are necessary for fruit production.

- **K- POTASSIUM:** The letter K represents potassium, as this is the chemical symbol for this element that is used in the periodic table of the elements. This nutrient improves the overall vigor of plants and aids in disease resistance.

Nature as is humanly possible. The timelines are the same whether you are growing indoors or out, so indoor conditions need to be a close match to outdoor conditions.

Sprouts and microgreens require almost no feeding since they are harvested and consumed when the plants are very young. Most herbs grow very well in nutrient-poor soil, with some being extremely drought tolerant and even considered invasive when left to their own devices in a garden. Mint, for example, can overwhelm an outdoor garden bed but is quite perfect for a countertop garden.

Salad greens also do not require very much feeding, even though they will take a little longer to develop. Lettuce, kale, and swiss chard can be grown in a sterile soilless mix as well as root vegetables like potatoes, carrots, and beets.

However, tomatoes and peppers are heavy feeders and do require a regular feed program so that they can produce a good crop.

Although we will not go into great depth explaining all the nuances of plant nutrition, it is important that we touch on the topic. Plants require 16 essential nutrients for healthy development. While all the nutrients are equally important, each is required in a different amount. The essential elements are broken up into three categories: primary or macronutrients, secondary nutrients, and micronutrients.

The NPK designation stands for the three primary, or macronutrients plants most frequently need in the largest amounts. Secondary nutrients make up the next three most essential nutrients. They are calcium, magnesium, and sulfur. The next

Fertilizer essentially comes in two types: granular and liquid (generally concentrated). Liquid fertilizers tend to be faster-acting; granular is more long-lasting.

seven micronutrients required in trace amounts are boron, chlorine, copper, iron, manganese, molybdenum, and zinc. The micronutrients are needed in very small amounts, and their function in plant biology is complex. Some nutrients assist in the uptake of the macronutrients, while other assist in the formation of healthy cell walls, or contribute to the efficient production of chlorophyll.

Plants also need carbon, hydrogen, and oxygen in addition to the above-listed elements, but these three elements are easily obtained through air and water, so are not listed in commercially packaged fertilizers.

Nutrition is important to growing plants, and if it is ignored the effort to grow your own food will result in poor yields and a waste of time and money.

Many countertop gardening devices come with fertilizers that are specifically designed to work with that unit, which helps to take the guesswork out of feeding. If you are creating DIY countertop projects, though, you will need to establish a fertilizer or feed program yourself.

Be aware that there is not really an acknowledged "right" strategy for fertilizing your countertop garden. Experience will be your best guide. As with any industry, debates occur over this issue. Every gardener has his or her own recipes for growing successfully, and will vehemently defend them. Visit a Master Gardener's table at a garden center, and all three sages will offer three different methods to solve the same problem. None of them are wrong, but none of them are universally right, either.

Here is a list of commonly used organic fertilizers that you could use for growing indoors.

FISH FERTILIZER

This product is often called fish emulsion, and it is exactly what it sounds like: pulverized and liquefied fish parts, generally the non-edible byproducts of the fishing industry, used as fertilizer. I know what you are thinking: "What about the smell?" Yes, some of these do have an odor, but many fish fertilizers made today are odorless. However, more than one indoor gardener who keeps house cats has reported that their pets have an unusual interest in potted plants fertilized with fish emulsion. The benefits of this product are:

- **It's fully organic.**

- **Nontoxic and safe around children and pets.**

- **Makes use of recycled waste from the fishing industry.**

- **It's an all-purpose fertilizer suitable for both indoor and outdoor plants.**

- **Builds up soil with rich organic matter, increasing microbial activity essential in the delivery of nutrients to plants.**

- **It is a mild fertilizer that doesn't burn plants.**

- **It provides balanced nutrition of all essential nutrients.**

Depending on the mixing rates of the product you buy, adding a capful of fish fertilizer to a watering can makes it easy to apply. These products can also be applied as a foliar spray directly onto your plants' leaves. Take care with this method of spraying, and be sure to use an odorless product when using indoors—for obvious reasons.

Kelp and Seaweed Fertilizer

Plants from the ocean's garden are filled with nutrients that benefit plants grown above the tide. It is illegal in some places to harvest kelp and seaweed from the beaches, so before you take a bucket to the shoreline, be sure to look into local regulations.

Fortunately, landlubbers have a plethora of products to choose from, ranging from liquid

Most plant fertilizer—especially liquid fertilizer—is dissolved in water at a specific ratio and then given to the plants via a watering can.

concentrate to dehydrated powders. Kelp and seaweed are not high in K (potassium) but are stocked with other essential vitamins, minerals, and enzymes that fuel growth and improve disease resistance. Other benefits include:

- Improved yields for potatoes and tomatoes.

- Conditions and improves soils.

- Aids in seed germination.

- Promotes flower production.

- Organically derived plant nutrition.

These products can also be applied as a foliar spray to the leaves of plants for a quick growth boost when rapid size is needed. Again, use caution here if using on flowering plants, as the spray can stain blossoms.

Chemical fertilizers do not improve soil structure. Organic-based products such as seaweed, kelp, and fish fertilizer, however, do enrich the soil by adding beneficial microorganisms, as well as nutrients. That being said, they may not be enough to deliver nutrients quick enough for fast-growing plants, so it is advisable to use organic fertilizers in combination with fertilizers that will provide enough NPK for growth, especially when you're growing hydroponically and there is no soil available for plants to derive nutrients from.

Organic Fertilizers

Not all organic fertilizers are the same. Do the research when choosing fertilizers, since although the ingredients may all be beneficial, they may not be in a form that is readily available for the plants to take up—or at least not immediately. Different products have various ways of being processed, and this can affect the immediate degree of nutrition availability. Organic fertilizers that go through a fermenting process have taken the steps required for the feed to deliver immediate nutrition, so read the labels. For the long term, other organic fertilizers will still improve the soil and the microbial activity, but when planting in this soil for the first time, they will not provide the necessary nutrients short-season plants require.

Look for specific certifications or seals such as ECOCERT or Organic Materials Review Institute (OMRI) on the packaging to ensure organic approval. TOPO lists many commercially available fertilizers and their certifications online at www.theorganicpages.com/topo/index.html.

Worm Castings

This is also known as "worm poop." Yes, worm manure is created by these familiar little soil creatures as they work their way through composting debris. Their activity breaks down green waste into a usable form and returns it back to the soil, enriching it while improving aeration and water retention.

The way I can tell my compost heap is done "cooking" is when worm activity has significantly declined. Once they have done the work of turning waste into black gold, they move on to the fresh pile and begin their task there. Nature's miners create the balance between decay and growth, so be thankful when you see them in your garden.

Creating compost using bins or spinners is a topic in itself. Using worm bins—known as

Worms won't survive in your indoor garden. You can get their nutritive benefits by adding worm castings (see below) but it is difficult to replace the aerations benefits worms provide. *Shutterstock*

Worm castings look similar to coffee grounds and have an earthy smell.

vermicomposting—allows small-space gardeners to create their own mixes. More information on creating compost with kitchen scraps is available on the internet.

Worm castings can be bought in containers and used for indoor growing by mixing the earthy-smelling, coffee ground-like granules into the soil used for planting. A notable advantage is that worm castings don't burn plants, so there is no need to worry about adding too much to the potting mix.

Designing a Feeding Program

Developing a feeding program for indoor growing can be a little daunting. Growing devices that supply fertilizer with the kit will provide instructions on how much to use and how often. Beginners will appreciate these foolproof guides when starting an indoor growing program.

The most important thing to remember is that less is more when it comes to feeding plants. Too much fertilizer can lead to various problems, from burn to leggy growth, so reducing the recommend mixing rates to 50 percent for young plants is ideal.

When using a soil or soilless medium, adding a granular fertilizer to the potting mix, as well as boosting it with a liquid feed every few weeks, is a pattern that is easy to maintain. Hydroponically grown plants get fed constantly, since the roots sit in the liquid feed from the time plants are started to the moment they are harvested. Reducing the feed rate for plants grown through this method is ideal.

While researching, I received several countertop devices from various manufacturers, but didn't exactly follow the feed programs to the letter. Fresh water free of fertilizer was sometimes added when topping up a reservoir. This allowed me to space out the feed times, and my results seemed to be unaffected.

Mixing ratios can be weaker in the beginning when seedlings are just starting to sprout.

The only time I feed plants heavily is for flowering annuals, where it is recommended to feed every third watering to ensure vigorous growth and constant blooms. Tomatoes and peppers are heavy feeders as well, so anticipate feeding them on a weekly basis after they have at least four or five sets of leaves on them. You can boost green growth with a high N (nitrogen) fertilizer for the first couple of weeks, but then switch to a fertilizer with higher P (phosphorus) and K (potassium) for fruit development.

Air

Plants need air above and below to be healthy. Hydroponically grown vegetables also require oxygen, even though the roots live completely in a liquid solution. Developing an understanding of

Even roots grown in 100 percent liquid solution need oxygen. *Photo by Shelley Levis*

the importance of root function, as with most of the topics covered in this chapter, can be a complex process.

When grown in soil, plants produce roots that go out and seek nutrients and water. Some put on tap roots and go deep, while others go wide. Some do both. This depends on the type of plant and also depends on the environment in which it must grow. Mining the soil for essential nutrients expends a lot of energy. Hydroponically grown plants receive nutrients easily in their fertilizer solution and therefore put more energy into shoot growth, resulting in a faster growth rate.

When asked at the garden center for advice on the best time to plant a certain perennial or shrub, I explain to the customer that fall is by far the most ideal season to put their purchase into the ground. In spring, plants are shooting up, up, up, putting their energy into producing as much foliage as they can to grab as much available sunlight to begin the photosynthesis process. If they flower, this is even more so. Flowers equal fruit and seeds, which are the offspring of plants. If you think about it, producing hundreds or even thousands of "babies" requires an enormous amount of energy, so the plant's biologic function at this time is to grow up and to grow out.

However, once flower, fruit, and seed production are finished, the plant switches gears and puts all of its energy into root production to prepare itself for the long winter ahead. This reversal of going down, down, down leads to a strong root system, which is the basis of all healthy plants. For this reason, it's best to plant in early fall, after the flowering season is over but with enough growing time remaining for the plant to extend roots.

Roots need air too. Oxygen is easily available in soil as long as it isn't saturated. This is why overwatering plants is as lethal as underwatering them. A soggy wet substrate suffocates roots and leads to rot. When plants are grown hydroponically, specialized fertilizers add oxygen to the solution, so it is important to choose plant foods designed for this purpose. Another accommodation for the need for oxygen is to actually incorporate air into the solution chamber via a pump or a bubbler that percolates oxygen down into the root zone.

Above the soil line or root zone, fresh circulating air is important for the prevention of disease and to assist in strong growth for young seedlings. A small desk fan set on low can create a gentle breeze, providing just enough air flow without blowing the plants over.

When assisting people in the seedling department, I always ask them to imagine what would likely happen if I gave them an unexpected push on the shoulder. The sudden shove would likely topple them back, since they weren't not anticipating it. However, if I were to try it a second time, a person would be expecting it and would brace themselves, resisting the push and standing strong.

Although the mechanics for this adaptation are complex, plants behave in similar ways in growing environments. Trunks grow strong and roots anchor down in resistance to the constant wind passing through their branches and leaves. A young seedling pushing up out of the soil will condition itself to the moving air in its surroundings, resulting in a stronger, healthier plant.

Water

I will never forget the expression a professor once shared with our class back when I was a student and an aspiring horticulturist: "He who wields the watering wand, yields the profits." This statement stuck with me and has become a mantra I've repeated thousands of times in my training of new recruits at the garden center. I cannot stress enough the importance of this constant daily task to my employee team. Watering is an art and a skill that you develop over time. An experienced gardener can spot a flagging plant from across a greenhouse

Don't let plants wilt completely; they may bounce back, but if it happens too often the repeated stress will lead to death.

or across the yard, yet the part-timer watering right beside may not see that the plant is clearly distressed and in immediate need of a drink.

Like any well-practiced skill, once you have been watering plants for a while, knowing how much or how little moisture a plant requires becomes second nature to you. In the meantime, here are some tips on how to properly water plants:

- Seedlings require gentle watering when they first emerge. Use a spray bottle to mist the soil while they are tiny.

- Once seedlings have put on their second and third sets of leaves, soil will begin to dry out faster, so now you may dunk these in a water bin. Rest the tray on top of the surface of the water and allow it to gently sink as the soil uptakes moisture. Once the tray is hydrated, position it on an angle across the bin to drain out all the excess water before returning it back to its home.

- Use a watering can with a shower nozzle (called a "rose"). A soft gentle stream directed at the soil is ideal as young plants continue to grow.

- Allow the soil to dry out somewhat between waterings. Look for an ashy gray surface as an indicator, and check for moisture by sticking a finger down into the soil. Or, use a moisture meter stick—a very helpful accessory, especially for novices.

- Running the watering can between the rows so that water pours into the trays or pots from either side is better than going right over their heads. Tomatoes especially despise having their leaves wet, since watering this way quickly leads to fungal problems.

- If you accidently overwater, give the plants a few days to dry out. Wet, soggy soil not only leads to a plethora of bacterial issues, but fungus gnats are common household plant pests, and they thrive in damp environments.

- Hydroponically grown plants will require fresh water replacement every one to two weeks. They can get quite slimy sitting in a fertilizer solution, and changing the water also allows the roots to get some air.

- Tap water contains chlorine and many other chemicals that humans have adjusted to. Seedlings are not so tolerant. When watering young plants, allow the water you're going to use to sit for a few hours or even better, overnight, before watering. This practice is not unlike how you treat water being used for a fish tank—allowing the chlorine to dissipate out. Well water and rainwater collected using a rain barrel usually have none of the issues when it comes to chemically treated water and can be used immediately in most cases.

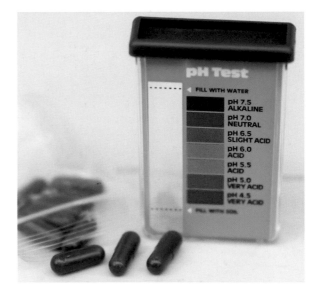

Water-testing kits like this one are easy to use.

Simple water tests are readily available and should be used before you get started to learn what elements may be present in your water. Truthfully, though, I have successfully started many plants from cuttings sitting in a glass of water poured straight from the tap.

I recall repotting a snake plant several years ago that was trying to escape out of its pot. I popped one of the divisions into a tall vase with a few decorative stones, filled it with water, and placed this in the low-light guest bathroom.

The only care this poor neglected plant received was flushing the vase with fresh water whenever the bathroom got cleaned. Air bubbles flowed in and around the roots and rocks, flushing out stagnant water and leaving trapped air bubbles behind. This method seemed to work for this soldier, as it held on and continued to grow for about five years before finally expiring, one mushy yellow leaf at a time.

While this example does not demonstrate a recommended practice for taking care of houseplants (actually, one might go so far as to call it plant abuse) it does demonstrate that plants adapt to their environments and can survive in some less-than-ideal situations quite well.

pH

These two little letters are just as important as the other three—NPK—discussed earlier. But what exactly do these letters stand for? The p is short for "power" (or potential) and the H is the element symbol for hydrogen. The term pH, then, means the power or potential of hydrogen.

The pH value is set according to a logarithm that measures hydrogen ion concentration of an aqueous solution. Basically, the pH scale measures acidity or alkalinity of a liquid solution. The scale runs from 1 to 14, with 7 being neutral, numbers lower than 7 representing acidity, and above 7 representing alkalinity.

Plants require specific levels of pH in order for them to take up nutrients. Most seem to survive well enough between 5.0 and 7.5—slightly acidic to neutral—but others generally prefer a more acid growing environment. Strawberries, cucumbers, and tomatoes lean more toward an acidic preference, while broccoli, cabbage, and onions like it more alkaline.

Measuring pH is quite simple and there are many ways to do it. Kits are easily available at local home hardware stores or garden centers. You can

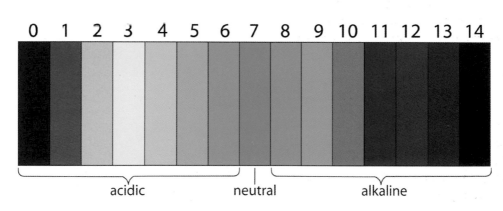

Shutterstock

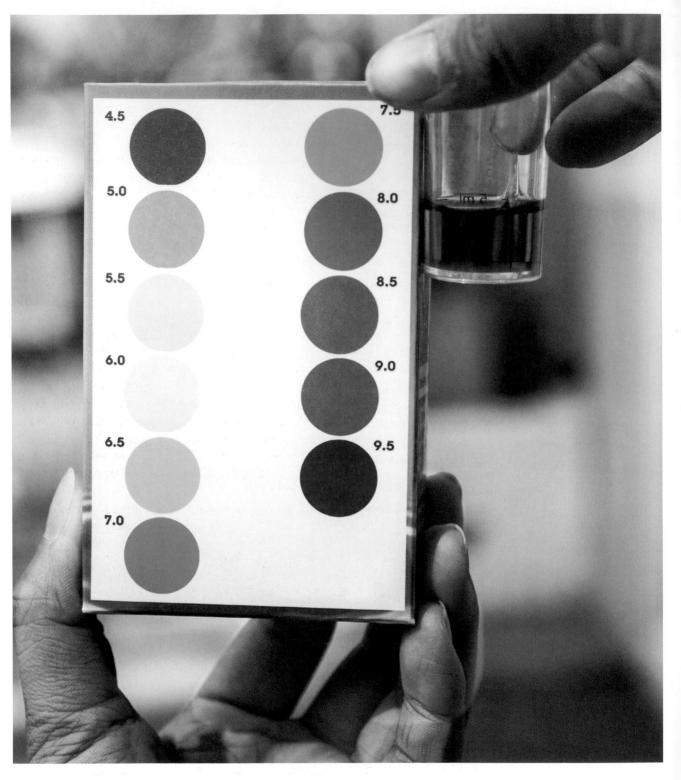

The pH of water can be measured with simple kits. The kit may consist of litmus strips or wands that change color; others, like this one, involve testing a water sample and comparing it to a color reference chart. *Shutterstock*

get test strips of litmus paper, or kits that use drops or test probes, with which you stick a wand into the solution. Soil tests require that you take a soil sample and swirl it in a jar with distilled water to obtain a liquid sample. Hydroponically grown plants only require a sample of their solution for a quick test.

Adjusting pH is also very simple—there are several chemicals available to the home gardener that are safe and easy to use.

Even the slightest bump on the scale from one number to the next affects how a plant can absorb nutrients. The fertilizer solution you provide may have everything the plant needs, but the pH level affects the plant's ability to grab it. A pH that rises above 6.5 can make some micronutrients begin to precipitate out of the solution and stick to the walls of the reservoir, rendering them useless for the plants.

Fortunately, dealing with pH is quite easy and most plants that are fit for indoor gardening sit in the middle of the chart.

Temperature

Most plants have an optimal temperature range and grow well between 58° and 86° F. Humans are most comfortable around the 72°- to 82°-F range, so indoor growing temperatures usually don't require much adjusting. Grow lights as well as heat mats can add heat to an area if a particularly cold room is being used for plant production.

To grow and to respire, plants require glucose, which is created in the photosynthesis phase. When light levels are really low for house plants, they cannot make the sugars required for them to grow. This results in stunted growth, and eventually starts a self-cannibalism process in which the plant begins to draw nutrients and sugars out of older leaves in order to feed newer ones, slowly turning the entire plant brown until it eventually dies. This is why people often struggle to keep plants alive in north-facing rooms of the house.

Cool-weather crops, such as lettuce, kale, and brassicas (cabbage, broccoli, and others), enjoy the early temperatures of spring and grow well during this period. As discussed earlier, lettuce bolts when long light days and the heat of summer kick in. Warm-weather crops, on the other hand, will become stunted when planted out into the garden too early, when night temperatures are dipping below 50° F.

When eager gardeners visit the nursery in early spring looking for annuals and tomatoes and such,

RESPIRE OR DIE

Temperature and light are copartners when it comes to the process of photosynthesis and respiration.

Respiration is yet another process vital to plants, and they must continuously perform this function or they will die. During the respiration cycle, plants use the stored glucose for the development of new tissues and to maintain existing ones. The chemical process of respiration can be read as:

GLUCOSE + OXYGEN → CARBON DIOXIDE + WATER (+ ENERGY)

If you look back to the photosynthesis equation we discussed earlier, you will notice that the equation for respiration is the reverse. Photosynthesis uses carbon dioxide and produces oxygen, while respiration does exactly the opposite. Plants constantly respire in dark or light, while they only photosynthesize in the light.

Once lettuce bolts and goes to flower, its leaves become bitter. *Photo by Shelley Levis*

I explain that planting out into the garden too soon will not result in bigger or better plants, but quite the opposite. Plants coming from an environmentally controlled greenhouse have been fooled into thinking that spring is upon them. They've enjoyed optimal light, heat, and nutrients artificially supplied in the exact right amounts. Then they come into a garden center, which, although usually not ideal, may have semitransparent roofs and ways to cover them up at night, accommodations that continue to fool them.

Taking a plant from this environment and moving it out to an exposed chilly garden with cold, wet soil and biting winds is going to put this plant into shock. Basically, the temperature and short-light days trigger the plants into thinking it must be fall. This in turn leads them to shut down and start reserving their sugars, instead of using them to produce more leaves. A few weeks later, as the sunlight increases and the temperatures begin to warm up, these plants need to reverse all over again, and may never put on good size or even flower by the time summer is over.

As a rule of thumb, I simply tell people that when it's comfortable for you to be outside in a T-shirt at night, then it's comfortable for these types of plants too.

Understanding how plants react to outdoor growing conditions of varying temperature and light allows us to take necessary measures for creating the optimal environment indoors. Vegetable crops can only grow outdoors during seasonal periods throughout the year. With artificial light and heat, controlling the climate indoors allows us to start a crop anytime, regardless of the weather or the season.

Humidity

The air in most homes sits at around 10 to 20 percent relative humidity, which is comfortable for humans. Plants prefer it to be higher, at around 50 percent, in order to keep their leaves turgid and remain otherwise happy. When humidity is really low, they begin to transpire at a rapid rate and lose moisture through their leaves, resulting in collapse.

Higher temperatures have an effect on humidity, since more water vapor can be held in the air as temperatures go up. Misting with a water bottle helps raise the humidity around plants temporarily, but is generally done too infrequently to maintain a good ongoing humidity level.

Living in the coastal Pacific Northwest, I have no problems with low humidity. I often joke that we

Misting plants may be adequate hydration in some very humid environments.

only have two seasons here—one wet and one hot, that's it. Since we have rain most of the year and the ocean drives humid air into the interior, we do not need to supplement this. In fact, I own a dehumidifier for when it gets really bad. Gardeners in my region claim they have webbed feet, and I believe them. But those of you in exceptionally dry areas should consider using a humidifier to improve conditions ideal for growing plants indoors.

And Now for the Good Stuff

This review of the basics was necessary to build an understanding of how many factors are involved in growing successfully. These are complex subjects, and this chapter has barely scratched the surface, though it should provide adequate preparation for having success with the projects found in the following pages. This important thing to remember is that plants want to grow. If the science feels overly complicated, you can take a breath and know that plants have all of this all figured out. Your only challenge is to provide them with the right environment in which to do what they already know how to do.

BEST EDIBLES FOR COUNTERTOP GARDENS

Choosing vegetables for countertop gardens will depend on personal preference, available space, and, of course, exposure to light. While any plant can be started indoors and be grown in containers, each plant has specific needs.

I often have to explain to people seeking plants for their homes that what they've chosen simply won't do well indoors. Lavender, for instance, is one that I get asked about frequently. Very few perennials, shrubs, and trees do well indoors, since they have internal clocks that they go by to determine their growth and flowering cycles. In addition, pollination that naturally occurs in the garden is absent in an interior growing space.

Most plants that require "seasons" will not perform well indoors, where the environment remains static and unchanging, and most will eventually die. It is no surprise that most ornamental houseplants are tropical species, as these species are naturally adapted to conditions that are more or less constant. Plants native to temperate regions, though, have a tougher time thriving indoors.

They may be small but sprouts and microgreens are packed with flavor.

Tropical, citrus, and other plants that thrive in environments that never experience a frozen winter can do well in an unchanging interior environment. However, these can be very challenging for other reasons.

Plant junkies always want what they can't have. In the Pacific Northwest, for example, a popular plant request is the Meyer lemon tree. It is also the most frequently returned plant, usually within a couple months of purchase and delivered back to us in a garbage bag.

My warnings at the time of purchase always get ignored. "Where do citrus trees grow?" I ask customers excited at the idea of harvesting their own fresh lemons. Although it is highly unlikely that they will be able to recreate California conditions in their homes, folks still think that all they need to do is put the tree near a sunny window and the plant will do fine. But the Pacific Northwest is not very sunny, at least not for six months of the year.

Tropical plants are genetically programmed to grow year-round in their native areas. So, unless the right light and humidity—similar to their preferred environment—can be provided, those living north of the 37th parallel shouldn't attempt growing citrus trees indoors.

Houseplants fall into another category: they do not like the scorching rays of the sun on their leaves and instead prefer a bright, indirect light.

Walking through a tropical rainforest, you will discover a jungle of understory plants that are thriving in the protected environment below the waving fronds of giant palms and other tropical trees. Shards of sunlight penetrate through the canopy and create an ideal low- to bright-light environment below.

The lesson here is to think like the plant. Understanding where it comes from is the key to growing it successfully.

The seasonal plant category that includes annuals and most vegetables do not live year-round and instead mature and are harvested in a 3- to 6-month window. This makes it possible to grow certain vegetables indoors, however some vegetable plants will do better than others. Let's take a look at types of vegetables and their varieties suitable for countertop growing.

Sprouts and Microgreens

This category of countertop gardening specimens produces the quickest results, by far. Easy to grow in just 3 to 10 days, young fresh sprouts, shoots, or microgreens are perfect for a beginner. They don't require complicated equipment and require little space to grow.

Distinguishing a microgreen from a sprout isn't easy, and there is not even full agreement on the definitions. Different sources will refer to the same

Seeds specifically for sprouting should be used for safety.

thing different ways—pea shoots, for example, are sometimes called pea sprouts, while other authorities label them as microgreens.

For our purposes, here's how we will define sprouts:

• Sprouts are the infantile stage of a seedling.

• Sprouts are germinated seeds.

• The seed, its small roots, and first leaves are all consumed.

• Sprouts are grown hydroponically—they do not require soil, just water.

• Light is not necessary to produce sprouts.

• Sprouts are ready to eat in 3 to 7 days.

• Safe handling is a must—frequent rinses with fresh water are required.

• Sprouts are mild tasting.

Microgreens can be grown in just about any container that will hold growing medium. Sprouts generally require specialized vessels that let you rinse the seeds very frequently.

Microgreens are the next stage of growth of young seedlings where they begin to resemble the mature plant it will eventually become:

- Microgreens are grown in a solid medium, like soil or peat.

- They are harvested when they develop their first true leaves.

- Only the stems and shoots are consumed—they are harvested by clipping above the soil line.

- They require light to grow.

- Microgreens take as much as two weeks before being ready for harvest.

- They have more developed flavors—they can be sweet, tangy, or spicy.

- Considered safer to eat than sprouts, with less bacterial risk.

SPROUTS TO TRY

Start with sprouts you may already be familiar with. This way you will recognize what they should look like when they are ready for eating.

MUNG BEANS: These are the common bean sprouts you can buy at a grocery store. Very easy to produce in just 4 or 5 days. Use in stir fries and salads.

ALFALFA: These grow before your eyes in as little as 3 days. Very mild flavor and good for adding crunch to sandwiches and flatbreads.

RADISHES: The quickest of them all—these will sprout in just 2 days. They have a spicy flavor and are delicious when added to salads or tossed on top of a soup.

BROCCOLI: Semi-spicy flavor that takes 5 to 7 days to develop.

MICROGREENS TO TRY

Although these take longer to develop, they are still quick and easy to grow. Start a new batch every two weeks and you will have fresh microgreens throughout the month.

ARUGULA: This popular tangy microgreen perfectly complements salads and fish dishes. Takes up to 12 days before it can be harvested.

BEETS: 'Bulls Blood' beet microgreens are delicious and visually stunning with their red stems. They have a mild beet flavor and can be harvested between 11 and 21 days.

CRESS: It has a peppery flavor that is great with eggs or mayonnaise-based dressings. Harvest within 14 days.

MUSTARD: Makes a pungent and spicy addition to salads and sandwiches. Try 'Osaka Purple' or 'Red Giant'. Harvest in 14 to 16 days.

PEAS: 'Tom Thumb' is a delicious variety to try. These microgreens have an intense, delicious pea flavor. Harvest in 10 to 14 days.

With so many types of sprouts and microgreens to grow, the list is endless. After trying some of the above suggestions, discover some new favorites, such as carrots, popcorn shoots, sunflower greens, or garlic sprouts.

Growing Methods for Sprouts and Microgreens

Sprouts are generally grown in shallow trays or jars. These are available for purchase, but you can just as easily use common household kitchen items to produce the same results. Since sprouts only require moisture and no light, a rinse-and-drain method is used for most.

Flax and watercress sprouts are an exception—they are mucilaginous seeds that swell with a jelly-like coating once they are watered. These are grown in dishes on paper towel or seeding mats.

Pea shoots like 'Tom Thumb' are amazing when harvested in their microgreen stage and thrown into salads or stir-fries.

Enough water is added to the seeds to break their dormancy, and after that misting with plain water daily is all that is required for these seeds to grow.

Microgreens can be grown in any container and do not require very much soil, since they are only grown to the true leaf stage. Any peat-based sterile soil mix will do. Sowing is done by simply shaking the seeds on the surface of the soil, pressing them down gently for good contact, and misting until they begin to grow. Once the first two cotyledons develop, move to a sunny location, or put under a grow light. Continue to water as needed until ready to harvest.

More detailed methods of growing sprouts and microgreens are discussed in the next two chapters.

Classic English Egg and Cress Sandwich

4 eggs

2 tablespoons softened butter

4 tablespoons mayonnaise

2 tablespoons chives, finely chopped

Salt and fresh ground pepper

Dash of smoked paprika

8 slices of soft white bread

½ cup fresh chopped watercress

Hard-boil the eggs and peel them while they are still warm. Add the butter and mash. Stir in mayonnaise, spices, and chives. Spread onto four slices of bread. Top with the watercress and the other slices of bread. Remove the crusts and cut into triangles.

Salad Greens

The next category of vegetables suitable for countertop growing is lettuces and salad greens. These easy-to-grow vegetables require a little more care and patience than do sprouts and microgreens, but they also do well indoors. Most salad greens will tolerate some shade, making them ideal vegetable choices for the indoor garden.

ARUGULA: Yes, this was mentioned as a microgreen, but when it is allowed to grow on a little longer, arugula becomes leafier and is more substantial, suitable for a salad add-in. Grown even further, it can be added to hot dishes such as pasta or used in stir-fries. 'Rocket' and 'Astro' are two great varieties to try.

BEET GREENS: Beet tops are delicious all on their own. Try steaming them as you would spinach. 'Early Wonder Tall Top' and 'Bulls Blood' are two good varieties to grow for beet tops.

KALE: 'Lacinato' and 'Red Russian' are two varieties I like to grow. These can take up to 60 days to reach full maturity, but outer leaves can be harvested and added to salads or smoothies anytime.

MESCLUN GREENS: Basically, this is a mix of baby greens that can be harvested one leaf at a time or sheared down to 1 inch from the ground for the cut-and-come-again method. Mesclun greens will be sold in different mixes, ranging from spicy to mild. Some varieties are mixed together solely for gorgeous color, using red leafy greens and dark purple varieties. Others are combined for specific

Kale and lettuce greens growing happily together in the same unit. *Photo by Shelley Levis*

Four Basic Lettuce Types

ROMAINE: This type features upright stocky growth with crisp sweet leaves. 'Parris Island Cos' is a popular green variety, and for something different, try growing 'Cimmaron,' a red variety.

LOOSELEAF: This has delicate crinkled leaves in a loose rosette form. 'Grand Rapids' is a ruffled green variety and 'Red Sails' is a good red one to try.

ROUNDHEAD: Roundhead lettuce has loosely packed head form with soft, thick leaves. Butterhead and Bibb varieties to try would be 'Speckled Butterhead' for its lovely red and green leaves and 'Tom Thumb', which forms the smallest head of all.

CRISPHEAD: These are iceberg types that grow with tightly wrapped heads. 'Jester' is a semi-savoy variety to grow; it has beautiful burgundy speckles on the leaves.

Lettuce comes in many types and varieties. Try growing one that you wouldn't find at a grocery store for a change of pace.

culinary flavors, such as an Asian mix that includes pac choi and mustard greens.

LETTUCE: With hundreds of varieties to choose from, it's hard to select just a few. If you are a salad muncher, try growing several types as well as different varieties. Looseleaf and romaine are more ideal for growing indoors, since leaves can be harvested one by one. Butterhead lettuces do well when grown hydroponically, but crisphead lettuces that form tightly wrapped heads are best grown outdoors.

MUSTARD GREENS: Mizuna, komatsuna, and tah tsai fall in this category of greens. Spicy and robust in flavor, they can be harvested as baby greens or grown on for adding to stir-fries and soups. Enjoy these raw or steamed. Good varieties to try are 'Red Dragon Mizuna' or 'Komatsuna Green.'

SPINACH: Known for its soft tender leaves and high nutritional value, spinach can be grown indoors and harvested leaf-by-leaf to add to salads. 'Catalina' is a good variety to try.

SWISS CHARD: This is the same species as beet root and can be used fresh in salads or cooked like spinach. Popular varieties include 'Magenta Sunset' and 'Bright Lights'.

Salad Green Growing Methods

Greens and lettuces grow wonderfully in containers. They are shallow-rooted, so a depth of 6 to 8 inches of soil is usually sufficient. When growing baby greens or a mesclun mix, the seeds can just be sprinkled over the soil and pressed in. Grab a handful of dry peat and just fluff this through your hands over the seeds to barely cover them.

I've found in my experience of sowing thousands and thousands of seeds that you don't want to bury seeds too deeply. In nature, these plants multiply as their seeds scatter to the wind and they grow where they land. Less is more when it comes to sowing seeds into soil

TIP!

For perfectly seeded rows, try this trick. Using a long round stick such as a bamboo stake (or a pencil if sowing seeds into smaller containers), lay it lengthwise onto the surface of the soil and gently press down to create a half-moon indentation. Sprinkle the seeds in the line and, using your fingers, squeeze the soil together to cover.

Keeping lettuce watered well is important for flavor—if it gets too dry too often, it will become bitter. When planting transplants, it's a good idea to mist the young seedlings until they get a chance to put down some new roots.

Kale and lettuces such as roundhead, romaine, and looseleaf do well when grown hydroponically. The tender leaves of varieties that are meant to be harvested when they are young or by the cut-and-come-again method are best grown with their feet rooted in soil for stability. These include spinach, Swiss chard, and beets, as well.

Alliums

This is a big family of aromatic vegetables, with some varieties that can be grown indoors. Included in this genus are garlic, chives, scallions, shallots, leeks, ramps, pearl onions, and yellow, white, and red onions.

Onions are a staple in cuisines around the world and range in pungency from the delicately flavored leek to the eye-watering sharpness of a red onion. Onions can also be categorized as short-day or long-day plants, as discussed in the previous chapter. Short-day types are better grown in the South; long-day types are better for growing in the North. Onions are grown from seed, sets, or transplants.

Three Ways to Start Onions

ONION SETS: These are tiny bulbs that were grown from seed but harvested and forced into dormancy when young, then packaged for sale. The rooted ends of the sets are pushed into the ground, leaving the pointed end uncovered. They offer the easiest way to grow large onions intended for storage.

TRANSPLANTS: These are sold in bare root bundles for planting into the garden bed.

SEEDS: Bunching onions, scallions, and chives are best grown from seed, since they mature earlier than other varieties and therefore are the best choice for indoor growing.

Onions can be started three ways: from sets (shown above), transplants, or seeds.

CHIVES: Grown from seed, chives will grow well on their own in a container placed in a sunny window. Or, try adding them to a mesclun mix.

BUNCHING ONIONS: These are also known as spring onions or green onions. They can be grown from seed or even be regrown from a bunch purchased from the grocery store. Simply snip the green part from the white part, leaving the roots intact. Place the white rooted end in a glass of water on a windowsill and snip the fresh green shoots as they grow. Refresh the water every couple of days.

GARLIC GREENS: Growing heads of garlic must be done outside, since like other bulbs, they require several weeks of cold dormancy to trigger flowering (known as garlic scapes) that leads to bulb development. However, garlic greens can be grown from cloves indoors. Plant 4 or 5 cloves into a good potting mix, place the container in a sunny location, and water when dry. Garlic greens will grow in as little as 7 days. Snip and enjoy.

Root Vegetables

Several root vegetables can be grown on a countertop or windowsill. Keep in mind that adequate depth and space are required for roots to grow successfully. Even though they are grown underground, the vegetable tops still need sunlight in order to send energy to the developing vegetable below.

Radishes grow quickly and can be harvested in as early as 22 days. Crowding these into a small container will work fine if you thin out the seedlings as they grow. Use them in your meals, and you will benefit from the sprouts as well as the radishes themselves as they put on size.

Considering how much time it takes to grow just a few carrots or beets, it may not be worth the effort. However, if you do decide to grow these types of vegetables indoors, it's best to choose compact varieties that don't require much soil depth.

Again, you can use the leafy portions of thinned carrots as micro-greens and the beets as sprouts, making the planters serve double duty.

Here are some exciting root crops you can try growing at home:

CARROTS: Short or round varieties will do best in shallow soils and containers. 'Romeo' is a round radish-style carrot that is rich in flavor. 'Babette' only grows to 3 to 4 inches long and is perfect for growing in small spaces.

RADISHES: 'Easter Egg' radishes are red, white, or purple. If you are willing to give up counter space to grow radishes, then choose something you wouldn't find at the grocery store. Harvest them in about 30 days.

BEETS: Beets prefer full sun but will grow in part shade. Cooler temperatures are best for beets, and they do not require much water, only about 1 inch per week. For something different, try growing

Gourmet potatoes *can* be grown indoors!

Shutterstock

Radish Salad Topper

¼ cup sour cream

 5 medium radishes, sliced thin

¼ teaspoon white wine vinegar

Salt and fresh ground pepper

Dash or two of hot sauce

Serve on a bed of mesclun greens for a light side salad, or as a topping with sliced roast beef on toasted baguette rounds.

Chioggia for their pink, candy-striped centers or golden beets for a lovely yellow variety.

POTATOES: These vegetables can be grown in bags and containers quite easily. Buy certified seed potatoes and be sure to 'chit' them in a sunny window for 2 to 4 weeks before planting them. Potatoes will form hard green sprouts when exposed to light, which prepares them for planting in soil. Two varieties that grow well in containers are the yellow-fleshed 'Jazzy' potatoes and 'Purple Magic.' The technique for planting potatoes indoors is discussed in the next chapter.

Fruit Vegetables

Some people are surprised to learn that some "vegetables" are considered fruits. How is this defined? Basically, if the food produced from a plant contains seeds, then it is a fruit. Beans, corn, pumpkins, and cucumbers are among those included in this category. So are the following plants that can be grown on a countertop indoors:

STRAWBERRIES: There are several types of strawberries: June-bearing, everbearing, and day-neutral.

June-bearing has one big crop in spring, everbearing produces from spring until the end of summer, and day-neutral produces up to three times from early spring to late August. The best indoor-growing variety is alpine strawberries. These wild strawberries are small but very flavorful.

TOMATOES: Large-fruiting varieties are not ideal for countertop gardening because they require a lot of room, heat, and sunlight to reach their final size and maturity. However, cherry tomato variet-

Determinate Tomatoes

Determinate tomatoes are compact and work best indoors; indeterminate tomatoes grow long vines and require much more space.

ies can do very well indoors. 'Tumbling Tom' and 'Micro Tom' are two good varieties to try.

PEPPERS: Hot peppers, such as chilies and jalapenos, are the best options for countertop gardening. Growing bell types is an option, too, if you have the room and the right lighting.

Mushrooms

These delicacies are surprisingly easy to grow indoors and require little maintenance except for constant moisture. Different mushrooms require specific growing mediums, but luckily there are many mushroom-growing kits available today. Since most mushrooms prefer dark, cool, and moist environments, this is an edible that can be grown under a counter without taking up space in

Alpine strawberries may be small compared to other varieties, but they are flavorful. *Shutterstock*

Smaller hot peppers do well indoors.

These oyster mushrooms from the Back to the Roots kit grow before your eyes in just a few days, right in their package. *Photo courtesy Back to the Roots*

the kitchen. Some common mushrooms you can grow at home are:

- Oyster
- Shiitake
- Portobello
- Crimini
- White button

Depending on the variety, mushrooms can grow in as little as a few days once the buttons have formed. If you love mushrooms, it's worth trying to grow some at home.

Herbs

Herbs are the easiest edible plants to grow indoors, in addition to sprouts and microgreens. I always try to encourage people who don't garden to at least try to grow some simple herbs for culinary purposes.

CILANTRO: This relatively short-term herb is a perfect candidate for succession cropping. Reseed often so you always have a fresh crop on the go. It prefers cooler temperatures and will grow in a part-shade situation. East-facing windows that get plenty of light in the morning will work for this herb.

BASIL: This grows fairly well indoors in a sunny window. Don't overwater basil, as fungal problems develop quickly in the plants when the soil is saturated. Pinch the tops often to encourage it to bush out.

CHIVES: Previously mentioned in the allium vegetables section, chives are considered an herb by most people.

Basil keeps well indoors as long as it is pinched back often and isn't overwatered. *Shutterstock*

OREGANO: This herb likes plenty of sun; a west-facing window is a good home for it.

PARSLEY: A staple herb to have at your fingertips, this herb likes full sun and does well in a south- or west-facing window.

ROSEMARY: This herb can be a little trickier than some to grow indoors. A Mediterranean native, it prefers hot sunny conditions and likes its soil on the dry side. It doesn't like its feet wet, so overwatering is the main reason it dies over winter, especially here in the rainy Pacific Northwest. If you can provide a grow light for this herb during short-day months, it's possible to grow rosemary indoors.

SAGE: Grow as you would rosemary; this herb loves the hot sun too.

THYME: There are two types of thyme: culinary and ornamental. The latter is the kind you see spilling over a rock garden or creeping between paver stones. Herb varieties prefer full sun and can get woody if not pruned back regularly.

GINGER: Not only is this a nice plant to grow indoors, but the leaves make a great tea and the roots can be used in your cooking. Ginger bought at the grocery store is chemically treated to prevent it from rooting out, so try to buy organic if possible. Soak before planting in a good-quality potting mix. Just cover a thumb-sized piece of rhizome with 1 inch of soil in a deep pot and keep it moist. It will take 6 to 8 weeks to sprout, so be patient. Place the plant in an indirect bright light location, and once it starts to shoot through the soil, hill it up to increase your yield, adding more soil as it grows. To harvest, pull up the plant by the green leaves and snap off a chunk of the root. Replace the remaining root piece back in the pot.

Ginger root will sprout into ornamental plants when planted in the right growing conditions.

Edible flowers like these calendulas are wonderful to grow indoors; not only can they be consumed but it's like having a living bouquet on your countertop.

Edible Flowers

I love flowering plants, especially edible ones. Growing them on your countertop to be enjoyed indoors is unbeatable for a plant lover. In the next chapter, I discuss one of the countertop units—the AeroGarden—that I have tested for growing edible flowers. Currently, it is sitting by my coffee pot in the kitchen and bursting with blooms.

I have to say, out of all of my indoor growing adventures experienced in the process of writing this book, this project is by far the prettiest one of them all. Each morning I'm greeted with the happy faces of my colorful blooms as I make a morning latte.

The edible flowers discussed here were specifically selected and designed to work with the AeroGarden kit. Other edible flowers will undoubtedly also work well with this system.

CALENDULA: Also known as pot marigold, this plant is a must in my garden every year. They grow effortlessly and continue to bloom all summer long. Growing them indoors has been equally successful in the hydroponic and grow-light unit. More info on how to use this edible flower is included in the growing devices section of this book.

SNAPDRAGON: This is growing in the unit and although not a premium edible flower because of its bland to bitter taste, it is safe to eat and can be used at least as a garnish for a special meal.

DIANTHUS: This flower goes by a couple of common names and may be referred to as *pinks* or *carnation*. An infusion of this flower can be used in cocktail recipes and in desserts.

Dianthus Syrup Recipe

Many flowers can be turned into simple syrups and added to recipes, drizzled over fresh fruit, or made into refreshing cocktails. *Dianthus caryophyllus* (clove pink) has a clove-scented spicy edible flower you might want to try.

1 cup fresh clove pink flowers

1 cup water

1 cup sugar

Remove the green calyx (base of flower) from the blossoms. Heat water and sugar to just boiling and remove from heat. Pour the syrup over the flowers in a heat-proof bowl and steep overnight. Strain the flowers and store the syrup in the refrigerator. Will keep for up to 2 weeks.

For a summer cocktail, add 1 to 2 ounces of syrup (depending on desired sweetness) to 1 ounce of vodka and top with soda over ice cubes with frozen petals.

Heirloom Species vs. GMO Varieties

Modified plants have a necessary place in the vegetable farming industry, though many people criticize them. But the reality is that our ancestors were manipulating the growth and performance of plants for generations before science labs began doing the same thing using faster methods.

In an effort to maximize crop yield or to improve the flavor of a vegetable in generations past, farmers took measures to save seeds or to force cross-pollination of different varietals. Some of the seeds from the previous season's best ears of corn were planted in a field with lesser-performing counterparts in hopes that cross-pollination would occur.

Grafting the rootstock of a rose that exhibits better disease resistance to one that has gorgeous blooms is another form of manipulation that we generally don't view as an abomination to God's creation. Why, then, do so many people have problems with modern scientific genetically modified organism (GMO) practices?

The concern over GMOs involves worry over the long-term effects of messing with the DNA of the plant. Certainly, if we start crossing species—if we were to put fish genes into tomatoes, for example—it might start to feel like we are crossing some lines. Our forefathers were just looking for a better corn, not an indestructible one.

The Difference Between a Hybrid and an Heirloom

Heirlooms are vegetable species that have been preserved, saved, and passed down for generations. Hybrids are a result of crossing two varieties of a plant to create an even more vigorous plant that produces better yields, or one that has some other desirable feature. Some hybrid tomatoes, for example, were bred to have a longer shelf life, a trait that benefited the food-growing and grocery industries.

Heirlooms are copies of the parent plant, while first-generation hybrids are a combination of two parents. Despite their current popularity, not all heirlooms are fantastic plants. They may lack flavor, have poor yields, or be terribly susceptible to disease. There is a reason why those hybrids were created, after all. Hybrids were an attempt at taking the best traits of two plants of the same family to create one super child. However, this in turn resulted in the disappearance of many old-time varieties, because the new and improved versions were ultimately better. Luckily, seed banks and home gardeners passionate about rediscovering some old favorites have brought about the heirloom revolution.

Production, travel, disease resistance, and storage are all things that are factored into farming of vegetables destined for grocery stores. From a business side, it makes sense to stock produce that can withstand all the rigors it will go through to make it to the shelf. This caused a certain homogenization to occur, in which great diversity of heirloom colors and traits were lost in favor of the familiar red tomatoes, orange carrots, yellow corn, red beets, and deep-green broccoli that dominate today's grocery shelves. It's hard to imagine that our grandparents and great-grandparents were familiar with purple broccoli, but when heirloom vegetables are introduced to the public today, some think these are the genetically modified ones.

I have this gorgeous corn called Glass Gem grown from seed purchased online a few years ago—an heirloom variety with the prettiest colors. It is a flint corn, which is intended for grinding or for popcorn, since it is so starchy. I use it ornamentally in my fall displays and have saved the seed every year from my harvests.

Heirloom tomatoes are extremely popular with gardeners (and eaters), but since most are indeterminate they tend to become too large and sprawling for indoor growing. Smaller hybrid plants like this bush cherry tomato can succeed indoors, and there are literally hundreds of cherry tomato varieties available from seed. *Photo by Shelley Levis*

It is a stunning vegetable, and once the image of it hit a thread on Pinterest, it went viral for weeks. It still gets picked up every few months, and my website stats spike for a few days. I regularly receive comments and emails about how I shouldn't be promoting GMO corn. Folks, this is the real thing—not all corn is yellow.

It is ironic that the genetically altered foods dominating the grocery shelves (I call it Frankenfood) doesn't require any warning labels, while food that is certified organic, local, non-GMO, or open-pollinated requires all sorts of descriptive text. It's only been recently that the heirloom varieties usually found at farmers' markets have become available in the organic section of the produce aisle.

At many farmers' markets and some better grocery stores, you'll find carrots are not just orange, just like tomatoes are not just red. Carrots range in color from white to purple to orange. Beet varieties can be yellow or pink. Tomatoes have an even more extensive kaleidoscope of color, stretching from almost black to orange, to yellow, green, pink, and purple.

Growing your own food, even if it is just a small amount on a countertop, means you get to experience vegetables that you would otherwise never find anywhere. Hunting for new vegetables to grow can be just as much fun as gardening itself.

A Google search for seed companies will return overwhelming results. Refine the search with phrases that include specific attributes, such as non-GMO, heirloom, or dwarf variety, and other considerations. Look for companies that have taken the Safe Seed Pledge, and be sure to support seed exchanges as these seed banks collect hard-to-find varieties.

What Makes Home-grown Vegetables Taste Different?

Someone once argued with me that a tomato picked from a backyard garden tasted the same as a tomato bought from a store. When I share this story at my speaking events, hardcore gardeners in the audience all begin to shake their heads in unison. No, that simply is not true.

Why, then, does a tomato grown in a garden taste so much better than a store-bought one? Its flavor depends on variety, ripeness, and even the time of day when it was picked. When picked from your garden, it's most likely organic and chemical-free, and it is as fresh as fresh can be since no time was wasted between garden and table. But besides all those obvious reasons, I will offer up my theory about why the food we grow ourselves tastes so much better.

Love.

That's right, I said love. When we start a garden, we spend time amending, weeding, and turning the soil, preparing it for the season. Seeds are planted, then carefully tended every day. We weed, water, and wait. At the first signs of emerging seeds beginning to push up through the ground, a little excitement stirs in us—they're coming.

We thin, weed, water, and wait some more. Finally, the time comes when we can pull up those roots or twist that tomato off the vine. We carry our treasures into our home with a sense of pride and accomplishment, slicing them up and serving them to our family. The first bites of our bounty are deeply satisfying in a way that no store-bought tomato could ever provide. It's not just the flavor we are enjoying—it's the wonderment of the food itself.

When we eat this way, we are consciously experiencing our food—actually connecting with it. Appreciation is heightened, since we know what went into creating that vegetable. It took months of patience, tending, and care. And that is the definition of love.

You don't need to have a big garden with a white picket fence to have this experience. All you need is a little space and some willingness to put in the effort.

I honestly believe that if everyone grew even just a little of their own food, we would not only be a healthier nation, but a happier one too.

OPPOSITE Some root vegetables like carrots and potatoes can be grown on countertops year-round. *Photo by Shelley Levis*

COUNTERTOP GROWING DEVICES

Today's advances in home growing have come a long way in just a few short years. Now there are literally thousands of products available to the homeowner or city dweller looking to grow fresh organic greens indoors.

This wasn't always the case. Years ago, I tried to turn the spare room of my small apartment into an indoor growing station and it quickly became nothing short of crazy lab experiment. The best indoor method I could devise required a bookcase and several fluorescent shop lights. Each lamp was fitted with one cool bulb and one warm one, to mimic a full spectrum of light required for plants to grow.

Watering was an ordeal in an apartment with solid wood floors. Long storage bins were placed on top of a tarp, and each tray was dunked into the fertilizer solution until fully absorbed.

Visiting relatives had to bunk in this room turned greenhouse when they came to town. I'm certain my future mother-in-law must have thought her son was engaged to a complete flake. This attempt to grow indoors had its fair share of difficulties and robbed valuable living space. However, the reward of being able to collect ingredients for meals from a shelf in a spare bedroom made it tolerable.

Green thumbs and newbies alike now have countless options to choose from when selecting equipment for indoor countertop gardening. Our desire for fresh, organic food available at our fingertips has caused producers to race to create grow-at-home kits that suit the needs of every individual, right down to the styles aimed at complementing different home decors.

This grow house by Modern Sprout comes with a light and fits perfectly on most any countertop. *Photo courtesy of Modern Sprout*

With so many options available, the first step in choosing the right device that will suit your requirements is to do an assessment of how growing your own food will work for you and your lifestyle.

Start by asking yourself these questions:

1. **WHAT TYPES OF EDIBLES DO I WISH TO GROW?** Are you a salad muncher, a smoothie maker, or a recipe creator? What vegetables, herbs, or greens are you looking to grow? When first starting this adventure, it's best to "grow what you know," then experiment with one or two new kinds of vegetables.

2. **WHAT KIND OF SPACE DO I HAVE?** Where will a countertop garden fit? Are you able to use a window? Several windows? Vertical growing above a countertop may be an option as well, if there is a lack of horizontal square inches available. If you can't grow wide, grow up.

3. **WHAT IS MY LEVEL OF EXPERIENCE?** Based on your gardening experience, rate yourself on a scale of 1 to 10 to determine what kind of device would best suit your level of knowledge. Being honest about your skill set is important so that you don't take on more than you can handle. The goal is to learn as you grow.

4. **WHAT IS MY PREFERRED STYLE?** Do you prefer a modern design that will match your home decor? Indoor gardening setups come in several different styles, but don't allow yourself to get too hung up on how a device looks. After all, growing indoors is about enjoying a healthy lifestyle, not just matching the growing unit to your appliances.

5. **WHAT IS MY PREFERRED GARDENING METHOD?** How do you want to grow your veggies? Do you wish to use soil or a soilless growing medium? Or maybe you'd rather stick to an all-liquid method and go hydroponic. All methods will give you results; it just depends on your personal preference.

6. **HOW MUCH TIME DO I HAVE TO GARDEN?** How many hours are you willing to commit to growing your own food each month? Does your schedule allow you to check in with your plants every day? Start small until you get a good handle on your time. (Of course, there isn't a gardener in the world who has ever taken this advice.)

7. **WHAT'S MY BUDGET?** If saving money is the main reason for growing your own vegetables, finding a device that meets your budget may be important. Factor in what you would be saving on buying food from the market or grocery store—some items that cost more store-bought, such as specialty greens, may be the types you wish to grow.

Make a list with columns with all of your requirements down the left side when you begin the search for a device that will work for you. Then list the devices that most interest you horizontally along the top. Work your way through the list and note which growing devices satisfy both your both requirements and your interest.

This time spent narrowing down your options will save you money and aggravation later. Startup costs of getting a home garden system can quickly escalate, and a device that is beyond your skill level or available time requirements will only lead to disappointment and failure.

To gather information on some of the different types of home growing kits available, I reached out to companies that produce them and requested samples. In this chapter I will share my experiences and the results from my trials.

The easiest methods for growing your own greens require very little space or expertise. There is a tradeoff, however, in that you will not be able to produce very much food all at once. However,

With so many devices available, it's important to take the time to decide what your growing needs are before you buy. *Photo by Shelley Levis*

these solutions might suit your needs just fine, especially if all you want are a few fresh herbs for jazzing up a meal.

Glass Bottles and Jars

There is room on any countertop or windowsill for one of these. Glass bottles and jars are perfect for growing herbs and are easy to maintain. Leakproof sealed bottoms are great for countertops, but the key is to not overwater them. Most glass vessels are transparent or semitransparent, allowing you to see when the soil is moist. Still, overwatering is easy to do and roots will rot if they have to sit in a mucky bottom. Slowly add just enough water to see the soil become hydrated, but not so much that a pool forms at the base.

Bottle Tops

Bottle Bottoms

Delicious herbs and greens can be grown in vessels made by separating the top and bottom of a bottle.

THE GROW BOTTLE KIT

Recycled wine bottles by Potting Shed Creations are just as beautiful as they are functional. Herbs grow nicely in the inverted neck of the bottle, while the wool wicking system draws water up into the soilless mix.

The genius behind this creative up-cycled design is that the wine bottle can be used over and over again and never look the worse for wear. The cut edges of the bottle are extremely smooth and level, making this product safe and easy to use.

When I tried to make these grow bottles myself, I quickly learned that getting a perfect edge can be challenging. Several wine bottles later, it became obvious that even when achieving an even edge all the way around, free of jagged sharp notches, the process of sanding off the top left the bottle looking scratched. It became obvious that the cost of getting a professionally cut bottle is well worth it.

Plastic covers help retain moisture while seedlings sprout.

The wool wicking material in the bottle neck means you don't have to worry about watering this mini grow system.

After you set up your soil and seeds, cover the bottle with a plastic sandwich baggie or clear plastic wrap for a few days until the seedlings start to come up. Then you can move it to a bright sunny window.

This little herb grower on my windowsill quickly became one of my favorite morning sights. The wicking system works like a charm, and my basil is happy and healthy. Most impressive is how evenly the water is drawn up into the root zone, allowing the plant to take what it needs. The result was a basil plant that lasted for months, even with regular snippings. Each of my girlfriends will definitely be getting one of these for Christmas.

The Grow Bottle Kit comes complete with a wool wick, soilless mix, plant nutrient, and a cork coaster to rest your bottle on. You even get to choose which herb seeds you want to grow.

Colored jars are ideal for shielding tender roots from direct sunlight. Pretty and practical, this mason jar growing kit doubles as home décor. *Photo courtesy of Modern Sprout*

GARDEN JAR THREE PACK

I just love this Garden Jar Three Pack by Modern Sprout. First, what is there not to love about Mason jars? They come in three fabulous colors and all the ingredients to create a hydroponic grow system right there on your windowsill. Not only will this trio grow delicious herbs ready for plucking at your fingertips, but the glass jars will radiate gorgeous colors when backlit by the sun. It's like having an edible rainbow living in your window, and you get to eat from it every day.

The technology is simple. A net pot nestles into the top of the jar while the wick is plunged into the water below. You simply fill the net pot with the kit's recycled glass grow medium, top it off with some coco pith, and add seeds. The self-watering planter is then placed in a sunny window once the seedlings emerge and can be recycled in this manner repeatedly for a continuous supply of delicious fresh organic herbs.

This beautifully designed grow kit caught the attention of Oprah Winfrey and quickly became one of her favorite picks: if it's good enough for Oprah, then it's good enough. The herb seeds included in your trio garden jar pack are basil, parsley, and mint.

Heliotropism: To prevent your plants from bending toward the light, rotate the growing vessel a quarter turn daily. This will encourage even growth and allow the plants to receive adequate light all around.

hydroponic system sitting in empty plastic kitty litter containers. No, it wasn't pretty, but the tomatoes didn't mind. My best tomatoes came once I switched to this system, and I haven't ground-planted them since. You could grow these inside with a grow light using this method—although I would recommend a container different than the pastel pink Happy Cat bin I use.

GROW BAG FROM *POTTING SHED CREATIONS*

A delightful little grow bag is available from Potting Shed Creations. The wax-lined envelope grow bag kit comes with soil and your choice of herbs, vegetables, or even flower seeds. The front of the package also displays lovely artwork of the plant growing inside.

Simply tear open the bag, wet the soil, and sprinkle on the seeds. These leakproof bags are adorable on your counter, and they make great gifts for green thumbs.

Grow Bags

Available in numerous sizes and materials, grow bags are easy to use and can be neatly folded up and stored when not in use. Wax-lined paper or burlap bags are aesthetically stylish, while simple pop-up bags made from plastic or felt offer better durability for more substantial crops. Most types of bags used for growing have drainage holes, so remember that they will need to be paired with a saucer to protect surfaces from getting wet.

I went completely to black grow bags for my tomatoes a few years ago and created a makeshift

Adorable and edible, these little wax-lined paper envelopes are small enough to fit on any windowsill.

I grew these delicious oyster mushrooms right on my countertop. *Photo by Shelley Levis*

MUSHROOM KIT FROM *BACK TO THE ROOTS*

Gourmet mushrooms are a foodie favorite. The Back to the Roots company offers a Mushroom Farm kit that is fun and easy to grow. Children can enjoy being involved in the process, as well—even if it's just a cool science project for them.

One kit will sprout mushrooms for months, and the kit takes up little counter space. The easy-to-follow instructions require that you scrape the surface of the compost block and thoroughly soak the bag—mushrooms love water, so you can never overwater your crop.

Place the grow bag by a bright window with indirect light. They'll appreciate the fresh air of an open window, but will dry out if placed next to a heating or air conditioning vent. Keep misting, and in just a few days baby mushrooms will begin to sprout. Once your mushrooms have stopped doubling in size, you can harvest them by simply snapping them off in clusters from the grow bag.

To produce another crop, turn the bag around and repeat the process. This can be done several times, with the record being up to ten harvests from one kit!

When I made my first batch, it was mind-blowing how fast the mushrooms grew once the tiny buttons had formed. In fact, it kind of freaked my husband out a little bit—to him they resembled an alien life form since they grew so fast. One morning, when I returned home after stepping out for a few hours to do errands, I could actually see that they had grown significantly while I was away. They were delicious sautéed with red onion and served on grilled flatbread with fresh tarragon and goat cheese.

TOMATOES OR POTATOES IN GROW BAGS

You say tomato, I say *lycopersicum*. Okay, I'm showing off a little, but tomatoes and potatoes both belong to the *Solanum* genus and both can be grown in a bag. You just need to provide enough light. Thankfully, though, as we discussed in a previous chapter, this is easy to do with the lighting options available to the home gardener today.

Growing potatoes indoors in a bag inside will require a bigger footprint than a small paper envelope, but if you have the room, then go for it. A 20-gallon bag is the recommended size for growing potatoes. However, you can opt to grow a smaller number with just a 10-gallon bag.

Some growing bags are actually quite decorative, such as this burlap one with a botanical print. Black or gray felt bags are great, too, and they match well with most home interiors. Just be mindful that

fabric bags that are not lined will show rings from fertilizer deposits; they won't be as pretty on day 40 as when you first started.

Several potato varieties ideal for growing in containers are mentioned in the previous chapter. The standard method of hilling up still applies, even in a grow bag. Put a layer of soil in the bottom of the bag and place four to five seed potatoes on top. Add another layer of soil to cover the spuds. Once you see the leaves and stems begin to push up, add more soil so just the tops are exposed. Do this as they grow up and out of the top of the bag.

Beefsteak-type of tomatoes are not suited for indoor growing—they are sun lovers and need the heat of summer to put on size. However, many cherry-type tomatoes suit an indoor growing situation, provided they get enough light from a grow bulb or sunny window.

Decorative burlap grow bags are available if style is important to you.

TIP!

Potatoes don't need to be watered until they begin to grow. Just make sure that the soil isn't bone dry when you plant. Condition the soil by adding water and mixing it until it is moist, like a damp sponge.

A wicking system in this herb planter does the watering for you. *Photo by Shelley Levis*

Countertop Container Growing Systems

Just about any plant can be grown in a container. Besides just using pots, there are several products available that make efficient use of square inches. In some cases, it means *growing up* while in others, it is about *growing long*. These next few growing devices are great examples of space-saving options.

ALL-IN-ONE POTS

Elho produces a huge selection of gorgeous pots for indoor and outdoor growing. The Brussels Herbs All-In-1 pot is perfect for countertop herbs in the kitchen. This simple yet modern design features a built-in wicking system with a cotton cord. In addition, a pair of multiblade herb scissors rests in a convenient holder alongside the pot for quick snipping on the go.

My experience showed that if this pot of herbs was placed in a particularly hot, sunny window, I sometimes needed to wet it from above to supplement the required moisture, since the wick system is a bit small. Regardless of what wicking system you use, always be sure to check in on the soil to make certain it's not drying out. If it gets too dry, the osmosis action of drawing water up through the cording may stop.

Stacking planters like this one use a vertical growing solution to save space. *Photo by Shelley Levis*

Tiered systems use vertical space for growing large quantities of herbs or salad greens. Planters like these allow you to build from three to nine levels, growing up to 12 to 36 plants in just a few vertical feet!

Watering systems vary in these types of planters. Some actually come with a bottom reservoir with a pump that draws water up through the middle, with drip irrigation tubes running to each planting chamber to water at the roots. Others are very simple and just require watering from the top, which allows water to weep down from one section to the other. Be mindful of this type of watering, though—sometimes drainage holes become plugged, resulting in one growing chamber becoming waterlogged while the one directly below it is bone dry.

If you have the space, you can piece components together to create a living tower of edibles from floor to ceiling. The problem here is in providing adequate lighting, since there will always be a back, shaded side on a planter that is growing herbs on all sides. One solution may be to place the system onto a rotating lazy Susan rack to help swivel the plants around toward the light as required.

Microgreens grown on your windowsill are great to have on hand to add to salads and smoothies, and to garnish everyday meals. The great thing about microgreens is that they can be produced and consumed in just a couple of weeks, allowing you to repeat the cycle for fresh greens consistently throughout the month.

This sleek, modern design fits most windowsills. *Photo courtesy Potting Shed Creations*

Vegetable sprouts add lots of crunch to salads while spicy mixes are great sandwich-toppers.

GROW BOXES

A lot of grow boxes are too wide to sit on a windowsill ledge, but the one at left designed by the folks at Potting Shed Creations is slim enough to fit most window ledges while still having a clean, modern aesthetic. The Micro-Greens Gro-Box comes with your choice of spicy greens or vegetable greens. It includes soil and a gorgeous bamboo lid that doubles as a saucer.

Fill the box with soil, sprinkle on your seeds, and gently water or mist to wet the planter. Once the greens begin to sprout, they can be moved to a sunny window. Be sure to keep the soil at the consistency of a damp sponge, as it can quickly dry out sitting in the sun. Microgreens are snipped once the true leaves develop, which is done after the second and third sets of leaves form. The first sets of leaves are the *cotyledons*—the seed leaves that kick-start the plant. Snip the shoots just above the soil line and enjoy them in your recipes. Repeat the process again and again.

Sprouting times vary from 7 to 10 days, depending on temperatures. If you are growing during the winter months, you may wish to use a heating mat or place a light bulb near the box to help heat the area around the planter.

In my test, I tried the Micro-Green veggie mix with red Russian kale, mini-carrots, and 'Tom Thumb' peas. This adorable box made a great indoor planter and produced quick snacks to nibble on when doing my household chores. I absolutely enjoyed the pea shoots—they are very delicious and filled the box quickly.

Herbs and microgreens require very little space and are easy to grow in small, simple containers. Moving to bigger salad items such as kale and lettuces requires systems that can handle their nutritional needs, and provide adequate light and growing space for their roots and shoots. The next group of devices will cover soilless growing methods, as well as hydroponic and aquaponic systems.

Grow Domes and Grow Kit Systems

Choosing the right growing medium for your plants is discussed in an early chapter, where soilless mixtures were presented. Soilless mix can be used in a variety of growing devices, from simple pots to propagation trays, depending on what you plan to grow. You can choose to fill an entire seed tray with a soilless potting mix, or opt to use plastic cell inserts to separate the plants for ease of harvest.

Using the inserts allows you to do successive plantings by removing a cell when it's harvested and reseeding it into another tray to keep a regular cycle going if growing a lot of greens is required.

> ## TIP!
> Harvest in an organized fashion for successive growing. By removing a cell or clipping the greens from the back to the front, you can replace the next crop or reseed as you go for a continuous supply of fresh vegetables or herbs.

SUNBLASTER KITS

SunBlaster has several products that home gardeners can choose from based on their growing needs.

The Nano-Dome Greenhouse kit is the ideal growing kit for seed-starting or for microgreens. It comes with a heavy-duty black tray (no holes), an 18-inch SunBlaster T5HO Bulb with NanoTech Reflector, and a NanoDome designed to fit the light right in the lid.

The setup is fast and easy right out of the box, and having the right light already included takes the guesswork out of growing seedlings into young plants. A vertical garden is entirely possible with this system if you have the shelf space for it. Since the domes are designed to fit the lights, there is no need to secure the lights to an overhead support.

In addition, multiple domes can be laid beside each other horizontally since the domes have a unique H pattern that allows you to lay your lights across them for maximum lighting and more growing space.

You can buy just the SunBlaster lights in different sizes, as well. These come with mounting brackets if you wish to attach them under a counter or shelf.

I tried a couple of different growing methods for these domes and lights for my countertop gardening. The cells were used for microgreens, and the full trays were used for mesclun greens. I like to place a second black tray with holes for drainage purposes into trays with no holes. This allowed me to lift the upper tray out when watering in case standing water accumulated in the holding tray below. Root rot can happen quickly when young seedlings are sitting in saturated soil.

I have also used the domes to start seedlings in coco pellets and rockwool. Once these seedling pods put on roots, they are moved to a hydroponic growing system.

Simple growing kits like this one have integral lighting and drainage systems.

Growing several varieties of sprouts at a time allows you to switch up recipes on the fly.

THE MICRO GROW LIGHT GARDEN

For growing herbs and salad greens, the Micro Grow Light Garden by SunBlaster is the perfect countertop size for a small kitchen garden. The all-in-one light and growing kit includes an adjustable canopy, a capillary mat, and four reusable, sturdy growing trays. Being able to adjust the height of the canopy allows you to place the light close to the seedlings and move it as the plants grow.

For this mini garden, I felt arugula greens and cress were a perfect fit. I simply love arugula, and since I'm swapping out the trays to start new seedlings as the plants are harvested, this Micro Grow Light Garden gets lots of use.

I found that this mini system with its small light caused the seedlings along the outside edges of the grow trays to stretch toward the middle. Rotating the trays daily, moving the outside ones in and the inside ones out, resulted in even growing.

THE GROW LIGHT GARDEN

The Grow Light Garden by SunBlaster is a larger version of the Micro Grow Light Garden. This larger size is perfect for growing kales and lettuces, and its sturdy grow trays are extra long for batch growing of your favorite varieties. This also comes with an adjustable lid fitted with two 17-watt, high-output bulbs rated for up to 10,000 hours of use.

I have red Russian kale, Lacinato kale, 'Paris Isle' romaine, and Buttercrunch butterhead lettuce in my grow trays right now. The capillary mat that comes with the unit is working great at keeping plants consistently moist. Plastic risers sit in the hard tray over the top of the liquid solution; the mat is then draped over this raised shelf, with one edge dipped into the water below. The capillary action wicks the water up and across the entire mat. Water is pulled up into the soil through the bottom holes of the trays to provide constant moisture to the plants.

This simple wicking system is efficient and an important feature for those busy people who may forget to water their plants every day. Filling the reservoir once a week is all that is required in most cases. However, don't rely on this wicking system alone once the plants begin to put on size. It may be necessary to top-water occasionally. Remember, too, that the lighting also puts out heat that can dry the soil.

After using this unit several times to grow batches of kale, I found that the capillary mat became unusable by the third use. The mats are extremely absorbent, and since they remain wet all the time, algae and fungus gnats can become a problem. I was able to gently hose it off the first time, but later found that it began to break down and smell.

A replacement mat installed after every third batch will stave off pests and diseases. While you

A mix of lettuces can be grown in devices like this. *Photo courtesy of SunBlaster*

This little kit doubles as a potting tray and a growing dome. *Photo by Shelley Levis*

can look for a commercially made product to do this job, several layers of newspaper work just as well. The bonus is that newspaper doesn't attract the dreaded fungus gnat, and it can be thrown into the compost after use. The paper can last up to 30 days—more than enough time to establish young plants.

THE GREEN BASICS ALL-IN-ONE KIT

If you are looking for just a small compact growing dome and tray, Elho has the perfect size to get your seeds started. The Green Basics All-In-One grow kit is a compact vegetable and herb grower that comes with an extra-high dome so there is plenty of room for the plants to grow.

The vent at the top of the dome slides open to allow for better air circulation, and the durable tray can be used over and over again for continuous crops. This kit also doubles as a great potting station to keep soil off your counter and confined to the tray. It also comes with plant tags and a durable little scoop for soil.

This system by Hydrofarms is one of the simplest to use, requiring no electricity or pumps.

Hydroponic Grow Systems

Hydroponic systems come in all shapes and sizes, with all levels of required expertise. Choosing a hydroponic system that best suits your growing needs will require a little research; using the questionnaire at the beginning of this chapter can help you decide.

Some hydroponic systems allow you to directly sow seeds into the units, while others are best started from transplants. Starting seeds in rockwool or coco seed pellets in a seeding tray, as I did in the SunBlaster kits previously described, allows you to keep a continuous crop going, especially during times of the year when garden centers do not have bedding packs of fresh vegetables available.

SALAD BOX HYDROPONIC SALAD GARDEN KIT

No power is required for this simple Salad Box Hydroponic Salad Garden Kit by Hydrofarm. Grow up to eight plants at a time using the net pots in a fertilizer and water solution. The root balls of seedlings are wrapped in root wraps and placed into the net pots, making setup easy.

There are no pumps to hook up; the instructions are to change out the solution once every 1 to 2 weeks and to top up the removable reservoir with plain water, as needed.

For my test of this unit, I grew kale transplants. I rolled up the root balls in the root wrap and pushed them into the net pots, as per the instructions. Since this simple unit does not come with a light, I put it under one of the SunBlaster Nano T5HO bulbs.

Unfortunately, the results were not great. The kale began to flag and wither after about a week. Upon closer inspection, I discovered that the root balls were saturated and that a smell had developed in the solution below. My plants were beginning to rot.

Fortunately, this system just needed a little tweaking to work effectively. I removed the plants from the net pots and root wraps, and, after washing the saturated soil from the roots, I transferred them to a growing tray with fresh soil.

After cleaning out the salad box, I decided to submerge a small tabletop fountain pump into the freshly filled reservoir and set it to its lowest setting. This was then attached to a timer that ran for an hour several times a day. My theory was that the agitation of the water by the pump would move water, nutrients, and air around the roots for a much more healthy environment than that offered by standing water.

On the second attempt, I opted to try butterhead lettuce instead of kale. Butterhead lettuce from the grocery store comes in a plastic dome with its roots still attached—this is actually a hydroponically grown lettuce. Knowing that this lettuce already grows this way gave me confidence that it was a good vegetable to try while I got the adjustments right on this grow kit.

I gently washed away the soil from the roots of the transplants with a hose and water wand set on a soft spray, then set the bare roots into the net pots with clay pellets for support. (Do not use the clay pellets straight from the bag; instead, first rinse them very well.)

Healthy roots will appear white. If they are looking brown, your plants will not perform well.

Choose from several designer Three Pot Hydro Planter looks to complement your décor. *Photo courtesy of Modern Sprout*

The main problem was trying to grow these plants in soil while they were sitting in water. If you use transplants for a hydroponic system, make sure to wash the soil off of the roots; if you don't they will become oversaturated and rot.

I don't mind sharing the mistakes made while learning how to use these growing kits. Hopefully, these tips will help you avoid them and lead to quicker results! These small adjustments to this simple unit were easy to do and were cost-effective. Now my plants are happily growing and I can give myself a pat on the back for coming up with a system that makes this unit rock. Plus, this lightweight grow box only takes up 22 inches on a countertop, making it ideal for small spaces.

THREE POT HYDRO PLANTER

Great design meets decor in this Three Pot Hydro Planter by Modern Sprout. Growing your own food never looked so good! Several color options are available in this hydroponic system that includes an air pump and programmable timer.

Three separate plants receive water and nutrients directly to their roots, while all of the electronics are neatly disguised inside the box. The components (all American-made) are designed to save water, space, and energy; and the only time needed is that necessary to switch out the solution once every 1 to 2 weeks.

No lighting is included with this unit, but it can be easily partnered with a grow light or set on a sunny windowsill.

Not only does this line of AeroGardens include various features, you can choose a color to match your kitchen.

Just choose your favorite combos and pop in the seed pods—and you're ready to grow.

Grow herbs, vegetables, and even edible flowers in an AeroGarden with minimal effort.

AEROGARDENS

Miracle-Gro has come up with an entire line of indoor hydroponic gardening systems. The AeroGardens line has several different features to choose from, depending on what your growing needs are and how "techie" you wish to be.

Models vary from advanced Wi-Fi notification systems growing up to nine plants to compact units that grow three plants. All the AeroGardens have lights with adjustable canopies, and most come in your choice of stainless steel or durable plastic. If design is important, you will appreciate that a variety of colors are available to match any kitchen.

If all those choices and features were not enough options for choosing an AeroGarden, wait till you check out the seed pod kits. Depending on which unit you get, you can choose three-, six-, or nine-pod kits that have delicious combos of herbs, salad greens, or even flowers.

Or, try their Green Smoothie Seed Pod kit, which includes a blend of kale, mustard greens, and beet greens. The Italian Herb Seed Pod Kit has a variety of flavors, including mint, savory, oregano, and basil.

Shelley's Easy Calendula Oil Recipe

Calendula is best known for its antibacterial and anti-inflammatory properties, making it ideal for healing salves and teas.

I love using edible flowers in my recipes—there is something pleasingly decadent about serving a plant's most beautiful expression to dinner guests. Herbal oils and vinegars are so easy to make, and calendula (also known as pot marigold) is one of the most versatile flowers of them all. Use the petals alone to decorate herbal butters and cheese logs, sprinkle them on salads, or make a simple cup of tea.

This infused oil recipe can be used for dipping fresh bread, combined with vinegars for a spritely salad dressing, or blended in as an ingredient in hand salves or other beauty products.

Harvest calendula when the flowers are fully open, free of moisture, and have no blemishes.

Pull the petals off the head and dry on a sheet of newspaper in a well-ventilated room, fluffing the batch once a day to ensure proper air circulation and drying.

Once dry, pack a small jar half full of the petals and just cover with good-quality oil. I like to use avocado oil, since it does not have an overpowering flavor. Flavored oils are best when infused by the sun, so put it in a sunny windowsill for about two weeks.

When it's time to use it, pour the oil through a strainer to remove the petals, then store in a tightly closed jar in a cupboard. Use it as described above, or experiment by substituting it out for other oils in your everyday recipes.

I particularly liked how these systems removed the guesswork out of picking varieties of tomatoes and peppers suited for growing indoors. The custom pods are available in combos of six varieties and are set and ready to go. All you need to do is pop them in and grow. Love edible flowers? They have those too!

GROW ANYTHING SEED POD KITS

Perhaps you have your own favorite varieties of seeds you like to grow. The Grow Anything Seed Pod Kits let you add your own seeds so you can customize your garden based on what you love to eat the most.

My experience so far with the AeroGarden has been great. Setup was simple and the unit is very petite, making it ideal for a small kitchen. The LED programmable screen allows you to select what you're growing and then automatically sets the appropriate number of hours that plant requires for optimal growth. It keeps track of how many days since you planted and when to add more fertilizer. It even monitors the water level and lets you know when you need to top it up.

These seed pods have little domes to protect young seedlings while they sprout.

I chose to grow edible flowers in one unit and tomatoes and peppers in the other. The seed pods themselves have instructions on placement in the unit; it's designed to keep taller varieties near the back and shorter ones near the front for ease of harvest and aesthetics. The pods also have other information on them, such as the germination times and plant names so you won't forget what plants you're growing.

Each seed pod comes with a mini plastic dome cover that is removed when the seedlings reach the top. The unit turns on the pump every few hours to circulate the water for a healthy root environment, and it is extremely quiet—only a slight trickle sound comes from the AeroGarden when it kicks on. The lamp portion is adjustable so you are able to keep moving it up a notch as your plants grow.

I found that the peppers and tomatoes slightly outgrew the maximum lamp adjustment and therefore pushed out to the sides. And I found that water levels quickly drop once the plants put on size and will need to be topped up frequently.

Overall, I adore this little growing unit. It's like veggie gardening in miniature and is quite enjoyable to set up. The design is brilliant, and the ease of use makes this a growing kit anyone can use with minimal effort. This unit is perfect for people who just want to grow their own food but don't have the time or the expertise to operate systems that require more gardening experience.

THE MEGAGARDEN

With the MegaGarden by Hydrofarm, we're moving into a hydroponic system intended to grow a lot of vegetables. There is some assembly required for this unit, as it has a water reservoir that houses the liquid fertilizer solution, and a pump designed to move the solution up to the second chamber where the plants grow.

The footprint is larger than those of the other devices mentioned in this chapter, but that means

Large lettuces grow well in these extra-large pots.

up and around your pots, providing the nutrients required for vigorous growth, then drains back down into the bottom chamber. This unit does not come with a grow light, so you will need to provide that with a separate lighting system.

The benefit to growing hydroponically is that plants will receive the nutrients quickly and efficiently to their roots rather than having to seek them out in soil. No extra energy is wasted in root growth as the plant can now focus on shoot growth. The result is that plants will grow faster, which means you get to enjoy them even sooner than with traditional growing methods.

Although this kit came with several parts and a pump requiring installation, it was very easy to put together. It does require room and a sturdy surface to rest on, so keep this in mind when selecting a unit of this type.

This unit is a classic hydroponic system used by big farms scaled down to a size perfect for the homeowner. *Photo courtesy of Hydrofarm*

more room for bigger crops. This is as close as you will get to the hydroponic systems used by large-scale vegetable growers.

Rockwool cubes and clay pebbles are the growing media; no soil or soilless mixes are required for this full hydroponic system. Rockwool cubes need to be thoroughly rinsed before you add seeds and begin propagation. Once your seedlings have put on their second sets of leaves, the cubes are then nestled into the clay pebbles inside the pots sitting in the top chamber.

When this top-growing box is placed on the bottom water-holding chamber, the water flows

The net pots are quite large, so growing tall types of greens such as romaine won't be an issue. Small drain plugs are located on the sides of the water chamber that make it easy to drain out the solution when it's time to replace it. Again, be certain of the placement of the MegaGarden in your home. Once filled with water, it will be too heavy to move, so be mindful that where you set it up is where you will service it.

The pump that is included is beefier than that of a small tabletop fountain. Always keep in mind that the pump must remain submerged in water when turned on, and that it must be unplugged when you drain the unit for refreshing. There is a water level indicator tube on the side that shows you if you need to add more water between scheduled change-outs. It also comes with a timer allowing the unit to turn off at night when you don't wish to hear the pump working.

I do like this hydroponic grow kit for the quantity of vegetables it can grow, but it does take up space and may not be ideal for a small kitchen. It is currently set up on a table in my spare room, growing leaf and romaine lettuce. HydroFarm routinely works on new designs, so check on their website for the latest in user-friendly countertop kits.

Aquaponics

Large aquaponic systems that grow both fish and plants can be complicated and are more advanced than most home gardeners may want. Creating the perfect ecosystem for both fish and plants does require some knowledge if you decide to use this method on a large scale. Aquaponic growing methods have been around for thousands of years, combining aquaculture with hydroponics to create a symbiotic environment between fish and plant.

Many introductions of aquaponic planters through Kickstarter and other crowd-funding websites never made it past the prototype phase.

Fish

The Water Garden 2.0 is not a large fish tank, which means that you need to choose fish that can be healthy in this environment. A single male betta fish is ideal for this garden, since they are known to fight with one another when more than one is present. If you wish to have several fish in the tank, then choose two or three zebra danios or male fancy guppies as alternative choices.

Fish that tend to grow rapidly, such as goldfish, will eventually need to move to a bigger tank. In addition, some fish require oxygen; since this is a low-oxygen tank, adding a water plant or an air stone may be necessary if you choose to go that route. Adding a snail or two that consumes algae will also improve the health of your tank.

A simple rule to remember when adding fish to a tank is: for every 1 inch of fish, a gallon of water is required.

However, Back to the Roots has a countertop unit that has gone through all the growing pains and is perfect for a small space kitchen.

WATER GARDEN 2.0

Kids will love the Water Garden 2.0 planter, since a live betta fish that shares its home with plants can become a kitchen pet. The fish tank has a fitted top chamber that recycles the water through the plant roots and back into the tank, providing nutrients to the plants and clean water to the fish.

Fish excrement contains ammonia, which is toxic to the fish when it builds up in the tank. This kit includes a beneficial nitrifying bacteria that is added to the pebbles used in the grow pots for the plants. This bacterium fixes itself to the roots and their surrounding area and converts ammonia-rich fish waste into nitrates the plants need to grow. The cycle then flushes clean water back into the fish tank, requiring fewer tank changes and a cleaner environment for your fish to live in.

You can dress up the tank with water plants that provide oxygen and other fun accessories for a cool underwater environment that makes this aquarium enjoyable to look at as well as productive.

The tank may require a heater for the fish if you live in an area that isn't normally warm throughout the year. A grow light for the plants may also be necessary as well, depending on where you put it. The kit comes with wheat grass and radish, which do not require much light to grow. In my tests, I used a hanging lamp with a grow light bulb suspended above the tank, since it was placed in a dimly lit area of the living room. I also put a salt rock lamp beside the tank to emit a little heat to warm the air around the area.

The kit comes with a 3-gallon tank, a grow bed, water pump, gravel, growstones, seeds, and plant pots. It also includes all-natural aquatic supplies for the water, including D-KLOR, Zym-Bac bacteria, and a pouch of Tidy Tank. All you need to do is select your fish.

Although I was never much interested in fish tanks, when I discovered that one could grow plants in such a device, the experiment became more interesting—and it quickly became personal.

I chose a male crowntail betta fish—and believe it or not, I named him Bert. I then put a couple of live aquatic plants in the gravel and added a marimo ball (which I named Ernie) to the aquarium. Marimo balls are living freshwater moss balls that just roll around on the bottom of the tank. I found that harvesting needs to be done in segments. There must always be at least one tray fully rooted in the grow chamber so that the bacteria continue to thrive.

The Water Garden 2.0 is, hands down, the most entertaining option for countertop gardening and a great conversation starter when guests come over.

Know Your Choices

This discussion has only scratched the surface of the choices currently available for devices and indoor growing units. Since new products explode onto the market constantly, be sure to take the time to shop around for the right device and look at all of your options. Having a small space doesn't limit your choices—you will be amazed at the advancements and the pure genius of some of the devices that are available.

Luckily, your out-of-town guests probably will not be forced to share a room with your vegetables, as mine did. Unless, of course, your goal is to have less frequent visits.

OPPOSITE Fish and flora live symbiotically in this aquaponic garden from Back to the Roots.

DIY COUNTERTOP GARDENING

Gardening gadgets like the ones discussed in Chapter 4 are fun and fairly simple to use. Certainly, the more advanced the device, the better the results will be in your growing adventures. But some may be a little excessive if you just want to grow a few herbs or greens. Before these devices came out on to the market, many contraptions were fashioned out of household items.

As a blogger who built an entire website using common things in uncommon ways, I love to challenge myself with DIY projects and share fun ideas that encourage people to think outside the pot.

I have one predominant thought whenever shopping or visiting a garage sale: "Can I put dirt in that?" Everything becomes a possible planter in my world, although not all of them turn out to be practical. When we start looking at things from a new perspective, ingenuity kicks in and something that was otherwise junk may get a new lease on life, reinvented as a planter.

In this chapter, we will explore how you can make your own growing devices with just a few simple materials. We'll work our way through quick and easy edibles like sprouts and move on to bigger plants like tomatoes and salad greens.

Open your mind to these suggestions and do a mental inventory on items you may already have on hand, looking for things that might work for countertop gardening.

DIY Sprouting

Sprouts are packed with nutrients and come in a variety of flavors, from mild to spicy. Have a batch growing at all times so you can quickly snip a few to add to a sandwich, throw into a salad, or jazz up a dip. Sprouts can dramatically change an everyday meal into something sensational without having to glop on extra sauce or extra calories for the sake of flavor.

Mason Jar Sprouting Method

This method is so quick and easy to do that you can make a fresh batch of sprouts each week. If you plan it right, you can start a jar a few days before a dinner party and have fresh sprouts ready to serve to your guests.

Easy-to-sprout mung beans or alfalfa are ideal for beginners. *Photo by Shelley Levis*

Choose seeds intended for sprouting from a supplier that labels them as free of pathogens and chemicals. *Salmonella* and *Escherichia coli* outbreaks have happened with commercially grown sprouts that were grown from contaminated seeds. As with any food preparation, it's important that you use clean and sanitary methods to avoid any unintentional illness outbreaks when growing and using sprouts.

Start with some easy seeds like alfalfa or mung beans if you are new to sprouting. These common sprouts are familiar and mild tasting. Move on to mustard and radish when you're ready to try sprouts that offer some zing.

WHAT YOU WILL NEED

- Mason jar
- Cheesecloth
- Rubber band
- Seeds for sprouting

1. In a clean, sterile Mason jar, add 1 to 2 tablespoons of seeds. Any large glass jar can be used to sprout seeds, so save those pickle jars and reuse them!
2. Cover the seeds with water and place a square of cheesecloth over the opening. If you are using a Mason jar, the metal ring can be used to secure the cloth. Otherwise, a

Swirling helps separate the seeds. *Photo by Shelley Levis*

In just 3 to 5 days, sprouts are ready to be eaten once they turn green.

rubber band will do the trick. Swirl the seeds around in the jar and drain the water out through the cheesecloth.

3. Add fresh water to cover the seeds again, and allow them to soak at room temperature for at least 8 hours or overnight. Read the seed packet, as soaking times may vary for different types of sprouts.

4. Drain the soaking water and give the seeds another rinse with fresh water. Drain as much water out as possible by placing the glass jar on an angle in a bowl or resting it in the sink drain. (The seeds cannot sit in water or they will rot.) Resting on an angle allows for water to weep out and for fresh air to circulate in.

5. Continue to rinse and drain the seeds in this matter several times a day as the sprouts grow. Sprouts do not need sunlight to grow, since they are the infant stage of a plant. Most seeds only take a few days—3 to 7 days on average—before being ready to harvest. They are ready to eat as soon as they begin to turn green.

6. When the sprouts are ready for harvest, give them one final rinse in a colander, then allow them to air dry and store in a covered bowl or clean fresh jar in the fridge. Most sprouts will last about a week; when timed right, a new batch can be ready just when the previous batch is exhausted.

Terra Cotta Saucer Method

Not all sprouts use the same method to grow. Mucilaginous seeds such as chia, arugula, cress, and flax work great using the terra cotta saucer method.

WHAT YOU WILL NEED

- Unglazed terra cotta saucer
- Misting bottle with water
- Muslin cloth or crop cover fabric
- Plastic saucer
- Seeds for sprouting

1. The rinse, drain, and repeat method is not used when you grow mucilaginous seeds. Depending on the size of the saucer, evenly distribute 1 to 3 tablespoons of seeds, then cover with at least 1.5 times as much water.

2. Allow the seeds to absorb the water and swell in size—it takes a few hours, usually. They become gummy and appear glossy as their seed coats imbibe moisture. Cover the saucer with muslin cloth or a square of crop cover fabric and move to a dark area on the countertop.

3. Mist daily using a water bottle. The seeds must not dry out, but don't allow them to sit in standing water that could cause them to rot. To ensure adequate moisture is being provided, a water-filled plastic saucer resting under the terra cotta works great—the clay saucer absorbs the moisture and keeps the batch from drying out.

4. In about 5 to 7 days, depending on the variety, sprouts will be ready to harvest.

Kids will enjoy misting this edible project daily.

Tiny sprouts add huge flavor to simple meals.

Fresh Tomato and Sprout Sandwich

1 small tomato, diced

1 avocado, diced

2 tablespoons fresh chopped basil or cilantro

1 tablespoon fresh snipped chives

¼ cup alfalfa sprouts

Squeeze of lime juice

Salt and pepper

Cream cheese

4 slices of grainy bread

Toss the first seven ingredients together in a bowl. Spread cream cheese onto slices of bread and top with the tomato and sprout salad mix.

(MAKES TWO SERVINGS)

Use cell packs to grow several varieties at once. *Photo by Shelley Levis*

Microgreen Planting Tray Method

Microgreens are the next stage of sprouts since they are grown on to develop roots and the first set of true leaves. These are grown in soil and clipped just above the soil line. Seeds commonly used for microgreens include peas, broccoli, beets, carrots, and mustard greens.

WHAT YOU WILL NEED

- 2 black trays without holes
- 1 black tray with holes
- Cell pack liner (optional)
- Soil
- Seeds for sprouting

1. You can choose to fill a black tray with holes with a thin layer of soil or use a cell pack liner. I like to use a tray with holes, since some sprouts take longer to grow than others. This allows me to pull the pack from the tray and start it in another tray for successive growing.

2. Sprinkle the seeds on top of the soil, pressing on them gently to ensure good contact. Mist the surface with water to thoroughly moisten the batch.

3. Place this tray into a tray with no holes. With this method, water won't seep out onto the countertop when you get past the misting stage and need to water the crop directly.

4. Cover the tray with an inverted black tray that has no holes for 2 to 3 days, until the seeds start to grow. Remove the cover as soon as you see the seeds break, as they can quickly become moldy if left too long.

5. Once the seedlings have their first seed leaves—the cotyledons—move the tray to a sunny window or put it under a grow light.

6. Harvest when the plants have developed their first two true leaves after the cotyledons. Add to your recipes and enjoy!

DIY Herbs

Sprouts are consumed as quickly as they are produced. All the nutrients required to grow micro-greens and sprouts are provided by the seed and the cotyledons, so fertilizing is not necessary. But growing larger plants such as salad greens and herbs will require a feeding program once they put on size. This can be done in one of two ways: adding an organic fertilizer to the soil when planting, or by using a liquid fertilizer when watering. A combination of both can be done, as well, but be sure to read the recommended rates on the product labels and reduce this to a weak solution for feeding seedlings and young plants.

Soda bottles can be upcycled as planters. *Photo by Shelley Levis*

Plastic Bottle Herb Planter

Plastic soda bottles are used often to grow greens. Many experts consider them safe enough, but make sure to check the recycling symbol on the bottle. Do not use bottles labeled with a 3, 6, or 7, as these contain forms of plastic that are known to outgas hazardous chemicals. And if you try this method, swap out for a new bottle each time you begin a fresh batch of herbs and recycle the old bottle.

A homemade wicking system provides water to roots. *Photo by Shelley Levis*

WHAT YOU WILL NEED

- Empty 2-liter plastic soda bottle
- A sharp knife or scissors
- Cotton cording
- Crop cover fabric, small square
- Soilless mix
- Herb transplants or seeds

1. Remove the label off the soda bottle and wash it in hot, soapy water.
2. Using a sharp knife, cut off the top one-third of the bottle, creating two pieces. The top, cone-shaped portion will be inverted into the bottom half that holds the water.
3. Cut a piece of the cotton cord long enough so that when doubled in half it will extend down through the top cone to touch the bottom of the lower segment bottle—the segment that holds the water. This will be the wicking system.
4. Folding the cord in half, push the looped end through the open screw top of the cone to about halfway up the cone-shaped segment. Cut a small square of crop cover fabric, then punch a small hole in the center. Push the wicking cord through this so that the cloth lies over the bottle cap opening. The fabric will prevent soilless mix from pouring through the hole into the water chamber.
5. Use the bottom half of the bottle to support the inverted cone, then add some soilless mix.
6. If you are using transplants, make certain that the root zone comes in contact with the rope by wrapping it around the root ball, adding more soil around the sides to support it. If starting from seeds, fill the cone with soil and sprinkle the seeds on top.

TIP!

Any natural-fiber cording will work, provided it wicks water. Some synthetic fibers will not move the water up through capillary action, so avoid them. Wool yarn or cotton cording works well. A capillary-matting material could be cut in long strips and used as the wicking cord.

Use a dilute liquid fertilizer once every third time you fill the bottle when growing herbs.

7. Once the cone is planted, add water with a fertilizer solution to the bottom half of the bottle, then replace the cone so that the cotton cording is immersed in the liquid. To avoid burn, always use a weak, diluted fertilizer to start young plants.

8. A transplant can be moved to a sunny window right away. Seeds, however, will require a misting of water and a few days under a plastic cover to begin sprouting. As soon as you see the first two seed leaves develop, the planter can be moved to a bright light source.

These stacked terra cotta pots are pinned with bamboo stakes to form a tower. *Photo by Shelley Levis*

Terra Cotta Stacking Planter

A popular method of stacking pots has made its rounds on Pinterest the last couple of years. Topsy Turvy planters are made by using a central support pole made of a strong material such as an iron rod and stacking the pots on an angle so they appear to be tipping over in each direction.

This method requires driving a rebar or other strong metal pole into the ground to support a large stack of pots. However, the design can be adapted for a smaller version that fits well on a countertop. This Topsy Turvy design is fun indeed, but can be difficult to water, since the angle of the pots can allow water to spill over the edge when it pools at the rim. If you desire a sleeker look and a planter that is easier to maintain, simply stacking the pots vertically from largest to smallest might be a better option for a countertop planter.

For this project, you can paint the terra cotta pots to match your decor or buy any pots that you prefer. I chose pots in a mocha terra cotta color, which paired well with the warm colors of my kitchen.

Choose pots that match your décor—or, you can paint your pots using an acrylic paint made for terra cotta. *Photo by Shelley Levis*

Growing from seed ensures full coverage in each tier. *All photos by Shelley Levis*

WHAT YOU WILL NEED

- 4 terra cotta pots, ranging in size from large to small
- Terra cotta saucer for the base pot
- Short bamboo support stake
- Soilless mix
- Herbs or mesclun green seeds (at least six)

1. The base pot will be the largest. A wide bowl shape works well as the first pot for a countertop version, since the second pot will sit flat in the center of the first pot. Mix soilless medium with a little organic granular fertilizer such worm castings, and fill the bottom pot. Tap the pot on a hard surface to settle the soil somewhat, so the second pot will not sink too far as the upper pots are added.

2. Place the second pot filled with soilless mix into the center of the base pot.

3. Push a bamboo stake through the drainage hole of the second pot through to the bottom of the drainage hole of the base pot until it hits the saucer. This will add some support to the stack and act as a guide for the upper pots. The stake should be tall enough to get through all the pots; it can be trimmed after the stack is done.

4. Add the next two pots to the stack, finishing with the smallest on top. Fill them with soilless mix as you go.

5. Now you can plant the herbs or micro-greens. If you're using transplants, the root balls will require space to fit around the pots. You may need to break these up somewhat to fit them in. If growing from seed, simply sprinkle the seeds around the soilless mix in each pot, being careful not to let the seeds drop down into the next pot—especially if you plan on seeding a different plant into each level.

6. Place the planter near a sunny window, or use a grow light.

Hanging Herb Planter

This vertical hanging planter is a perfect project for anywhere that space is an issue. A fun DIY project, the simple macramé hanger makes a decorative edible feature in the kitchen.

Watering this planter can be a bit messy if you choose not to use a drip tray in each pocket, so try using insert pots instead. Depending on the size of the terra cotta pot you choose, a 4-inch or 6-inch plastic pot wrapped with a plastic sandwich baggie can be slipped into each terra cotta pot to avoid spills.

WHAT YOU WILL NEED

- 3 terra cotta pots
- Acrylic paints (green and white)
- Lettered stencil
- Yarn or wool
- Macramé ring
- Soilless mix
- Herbs

1. Paint the pots in the color you desire with an acrylic paint intended for terra cotta pots. If you wish, have fun with a lettering stencil and name each pot for the herb it will contain.

2. Place each plastic potted herb into one of the terra cotta pots, then set it aside.

3. For the macramé hanger, choose a thick yarn or wool as bulky as you can find in your color preference. Cut three pieces, each about 4½ yards long. If you are using pots larger than 4 inches, add another ½ yard or so to allow for more length.

4. Take the ring (metal or wood) and slide it down until it's in the center of the yarn so that half of the strands are on either side, then make a simple square knot tied tightly to the ring.

5. You will now have six strands. Divide these into pairs, forming three sets of pairs. Hang the ring to something solid, as this will allow you to use gravity to set your lengths when you do the next few knots.

6. Now measure down 15 inches from the top knot and make another knot in the two strands hanging to the left. Repeat this with the middle and right pairs, making sure they are all approximately the same distance from the topknot.

7. Gather all six strands together and do another square knot, about 4 inches below the last three knots. This is the first pocket.

8. For the second pocket, measure 6 inches from the square knot. This provides room to insert the plant below the first pocket. (Again, adjust the lengths if you use bigger pots.) Divide the six strands into three pairs, and knot each pair again. Gather together, move down another 4 inches, and square-knot the six strands together.

9. For the last basket, measure 6 inches down and knot, then 4 inches down, repeating the steps above, finishing with a square knot. If you wish, add a wood bead or piece of driftwood at the end and put another square knot below to hold it in place.

10. Time to put potted herbs in the hanger. Space out the strands so that they securely hold the pots in place. Find a lovely window, hang from the ceiling, and enjoy!

Simple Creamy Cilantro Dressing

½ cup Greek yogurt

¾ cup cilantro leaves, loosely packed

2 garlic cloves, minced

Juice of 1 lime

Drizzle of olive oil

Salt and pepper to taste

Blend all ingredients in a food processor. If you plan to use this to top a Mexican dish, try adding a little heat with some diced jalapeno. Keeps in the refrigerator for 3 to 4 days.

Hang above a countertop to maximize the available vertical space. *Photo by Shelley Levis*

Mason Jar Self-Watering Planter

This project is similar to the Mason jar planter from Modern Sprout, but this DIY version uses a plastic net pot. If you are not able to find a net pot, try finding a large mesh tea strainer that will fit through the top of the Mason jar you are using.

WHAT YOU WILL NEED

- Large Mason jar
- Net pot (or tea strainer)
- Cotton cording
- Cover crop fabric, small piece (if needed)
- Soilless mix
- Herb transplant (or herb seeds)

1. If using a tea strainer, cut a small hole in the bottom.
2. Cut a piece of cotton cording so that, when folded in half, the length is long enough to stretch from the center of the net pot or strainer to the bottom of the jar.
3. Push the cotton cording up through the hole of the strainer or through the holes of the net pot so that it is sitting at least halfway in the middle of the pot.
4. Line the net pot with some cover crop fabric if the holes are large.
5. Add soilless mix, and plant the herb transplant. If you are using seeds instead, sprinkle them on the surface of the soil and press lightly to ensure good contact.
6. Fill the Mason jar with a fertilizer-water solution up to the bottom of where the net pot will reach.
7. Suspend the cotton cording down into the water, and place the net pot inside the jar.
8. If you planted seed, cover the top of the jar with a plastic baggie or wrap, and allow the seeds to sprout away from a bright light source.
9. Once the seeds sprout, remove the cover and place in a sunny location.
10. Add a weak fertilizer solution to the jar, as needed.

LEFT Mason jars are easily turned into simple hydroponic planters.
OPPOSITE Oregano and other herbs will grow nicely in this Mason jar setup.
Photos by Shelley Levis

Creative Containers for Salad Greens

Fresh greens can be grown continuously indoors throughout the year and harvested one leaf at a time.

Framed Vertical Planter

Why not make a work of art that is good enough to eat? This shadow box-style planter is designed to sit on a countertop, or it can be hung on the wall. Swiss chard, beet greens, or spinach work perfectly in this gorgeous edible planter.

WHAT YOU WILL NEED

- 1- × 3- x 6-inch cedar planks
- Wood glue
- Framing nails
- Drill and bits
- Long wood screws
- Framing nails or nail gun
- 10- x 10-inch square plastic liner
- Stapler
- Moss
- Fishing line or twine
- Soilless mix
- Beet greens, swiss chard, spinach

An edible work of art can either be set on a countertop or hung on a wall above.

1. Cut the cedar into the following lengths if you choose to make butted (nonmitered) ends: 2 pieces at 14½ inches long; 2 pieces at 10 inches long; and 4 pieces at 11½ inches long if you choose to avoid mitered ends. If you wish to miter the ends, then cut pieces at: 4 pieces at 14½ inches; and 4 pieces at 11½ inches long. The open-ended shadow box portion uses the 11½ -inch pieces. The others are for the frame, depending on the style you choose.

2. For a nonmitered frame, use wood glue and clamps to form a box with the longer 14½ inch pieces around the shorter 10-inch pieces. Let dry completely.
   Option: if you are mitering the corners, bevel-cut the ends of all pieces at 45 degrees, then use glue and clamps to hold the pieces together as a box. Allow the glue to dry.

3. For the shadow box, each end of the 11½-inch pieces will join to the other on a 90-degree angle to form a box. The end grain of each

The shadow box holds the plastic tray for planting.
Photo by Shelley Levis

board will be exposed, but this won't matter since this part is hidden.

4. Once the outer frame is dry, reinforce the glued joints by drilling pilot holes and driving long woods screws into each joined end. Use a long wood screw to reinforce the glued joined ends. Position the screws so that the exposed head will face the top and bottom of the box, not the sides.

5. Reinforce the shadow box in the same manner. This box will have screws on all four sides, but this will not matter since this portion is hidden.

6. Glue the shadow box onto the frame and allow to dry.

7. Once the glue is dry, use framing nails or a nail gun to reinforce the bond between the two.

8. Place the plastic liner inside the frame and use the twine to secure in place. Staple one piece from top to bottom and the other from side to side.

9. Put some soil into the liner and add some worm castings. Plant starter vegetables from transplant packs, arranging them in an artistic manner that shows off their color and texture.

10. Once planted, loosely add moss, working it gently between the plants to help secure the soil in place.

11. Secure the moss in place with twine or fishing line worked between the plants and stapled to the inside of the frame.

12. Water the planter, then position the frame flat in a sunny location for at least a week while the new plants put on roots.

13. Once the soil, moss, and plants appear settled and don't shift easily when the frame is tilted up on its side, the living wall art is ready to be hung.

14. Harvest by removing the outermost leaves as the plants grow.

Sautéed Beets and Goat Cheese

4 small beets, thinly sliced   Drizzle of olive oil
1½ cups beet greens   ¼ cup goat cheese
½ cup basil, chopped   Salt and pepper to taste
½ cup walnuts, chopped

Roast the chopped walnuts in a frying pan until browned. Remove from heat and put aside. Add olive oil and sliced beets, then sauté until slightly tender. Add the beet greens, and cover pan for a few minutes to wilt the greens.

Transfer the beets and beet greens to a bowl. Toss with a little more olive oil, basil, walnuts, salt, and pepper. Serve topped with crumbled goat cheese.

Suction Cup Window Planter

How about this project idea for a good way to upcycle an everyday object? Turn a dollar store suction cup caddy into a living window planter that can be enjoyed at eye level. If you have an unsightly view, these living edible planters might just make the perfect distraction. I found two plastic suction cup caddies at the dollar store for this project. There are metal ones available, but I found that the frame was too wide between the bars to securely keep the soil and plant intact. If you find a good metal caddie with a tight frame, then by all means use that if you prefer.

A pen caddy or any mesh-type small basket will work for this project, even if it does not have suction cups attached. Or, you can buy the suction cups separately, and turn anything into a suction cup planter.

Using a common object in uncommon ways.

WHAT YOU WILL NEED

- Small shower suction cup caddy, net pots, or any small container with holes

- Moss

- Suction cups (optional)

- Soilless mix

- Salad greens, chives, or herbs

TIP!

Indoor wall planters are best removed and placed in a sink for watering, in order to avoid water damage to surfaces. Once it's drained and dried off, return it to its place on the wall or window.

1. Use just enough moss to plug the holes of the caddy to prevent soilless mix from leaking through. It's best to wet the moss first so that it packs tighter when you do this step.

2. Once you have the moss liner in place, add some soil and a touch of worm castings.

3. Plant the caddy with a vegetable start, or seed the container.

4. Place in a sunny window and marvel at your upcycled creation. Now that's thinking outside the pot!

Once the planter has finished draining, return it to its spot on the window. *Photo by Shelley Levis*

Glass Jar Tomato Planter

You can grow a tomato plant in any large jar you choose. For this project, I found a large, inexpensive blue jar at a housewares store. The colored jar helps protect the roots from the sun's rays, and it will look fabulous as a decorative planter in the home.

If you have a large jar that happens to be clear, you can paint it any color you wish. I found that a good spray paint such as TREMCLAD works best, since it won't scrape off, as acrylics may do.

For watering I've chosen a funnel known as the Plant Nanny. There are several terra cotta watering funnels available for purchase. The Plant Nanny works like an olla pot, in which the simple pottery funnel holds the water and the soil absorbs it through osmosis. The soil draws the moisture from the apparatus as the plant draws water from the soil needed. This simple yet ingenious device has been around for centuries and is available in all size ranges to suit any pot.

WHAT YOU WILL NEED	
• Large decorative glass jar	• Empty condiment bottle
• Activated charcoal	• Soilless mix
• Terra cotta Plant Nanny	• Tomato transplant

Gorgeous jars make for interesting planters. *Photo by Shelley Levis*

Edible indoor countertop garden planters like this one make great houseplants too!

1. Start by putting down a layer of charcoal, available at garden centers. This layer helps prevent standing water from becoming sour and allows air to circulate below the root zone. Overwatering this type of planter is easy to do, but as I explain in the next few steps, this should never occur if you use a simple water delivery device.

2. Now add the soil layer, leaving room for the tomato plant. Add some organic fertilizer such as worm castings to the soil as you fill the jar.

3. Plant the tomato plant of your choice. Good candidates are compact cherry-type tomatoes and tumblers that don't grow very large.

4. Once the tomato is planted, push the terra cotta Plant Nanny into the soil to the side halfway between the plant and the rim of the jar.

Option: Some of the terra cotta funnels can hold a recycled wine bottle full of water. Once everything's planted, you can graduate to using a wine bottle. In the meantime, any small glass condiment bottle will work. Fill the bottle with water and invert it into the funnel. Refill as needed and watch how the plant waters itself.

5. Place the jar near a sunny window or under a grow light.

6. Use a liquid fertilizer solution as instructed to maximize the plant's performance and yield.

Plant Nanny

TIP!

If using a clear jar that you wish to paint, apply a piece of masking tape up along one side before you apply the color. When done, remove the tape—now you have a window to see into the jar to ensure that you are not overwatering the plant.

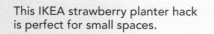

This IKEA strawberry planter hack
is perfect for small spaces.

IKEA Strawberry Planter

I came up with this idea while shopping at IKEA one day. This idea became a hit and went viral on Pinterest. Since creating it, I have given many demonstrations on how to make this small space vertical wall planter for under $10.

WHAT YOU WILL NEED

- IKEA Variera Plastic Bag Dispenser
- Moss
- Soilless mix
- 10-pack of strawberry runners

1. With the dispenser open and laying on a flat surface, spread the moss over the plastic to completely cover all the holes.

2. Top with soilless mix and organic fertilizer, spreading it over all of the exposed moss.

3. Roll up the end of the plastic dispenser and fasten it to the appropriate grooves as per the assembly instructions, and close up the bottom. Now it's ready to plant.

4. Separate the strawberry runners in the pack. Stuff the roots of a runner into every other hole, using your fingers to first separate the moss and then to pinch it around each runner to secure it in place.

5. Hang the planter on a sunny wall.

6. To water, take the planter down and place over the sink to water from the top. Once it's fully drained, return it to its spot on the wall.

The basic ingredients are some soilless mix and moss, a strawberry plant, and a hackable strawberry planter. *Photo by Shelley Levis*

After you make the layers of soilless mix and moss, roll it up and click it together. *Photo by Shelley Levis*

TIP!

Each strawberry plant contains all the reproductive parts needed to pollinate in each flower. However, grown indoors, they will lack the help they get outdoors from bees. To pollinate them yourself, simply rub two flowers gently together or use a small paintbrush to move pollen from the stamens to the yellow center of the flower. When the center begins to swell and the white petals shrivel up, the flower has successfully been pollinated and fruit will soon follow.

Be Creative

Almost anything can become a planter. Use your imagination and take a look at items that are already on hand around the house. For example, for years I stored a set of mini white ceramic condiment serving cups with a matching ceramic tray that we received as a wedding gift. One day I realized that by putting dirt in those little cups, I could make it into an adorable window planter for some succulents.

It now lives happily in a hot sunny window above my kitchen sink and is one of my most favorite planters.

But don't get too carried away and start potting up everything in sight. What may start off as a great idea can quickly turn into a begrudged watering chore later on. Plants need water, patience, and routine. If you can willingly provide this daily, then you will not have wasted your time or your money.

These little condiment serving cups sat unused for years before I realized I could make them into a window planter! You probably have similarly unused containers around your home that you can repurpose. *Photo by Shelley Levis*

TROUBLESHOOTING

Several problems can plague any attempt to grow vegetables, whether it is indoors or out. Even if every step to grow something is followed to the letter, crop failure, pests, or disease can still affect the results.

I often counsel folks who feel defeated because they just couldn't get a plant to survive, reminding them that plants bought from a store go through quite a bit of moving and jostling even before they make their way to your home.

Annuals and vegetable transplants suffer the most from heat and light fluctuations in early spring. Even transplants that are brought directly home from a nursery and put into an indoor growing device can become shocked from the changes in light and temperature.

Starting from seed ensures that the plant doesn't need constant adjusting, but this too has its own set of problems. While some of the troubleshooting suggestions on the following pages may answer your questions, this may not be enough to correct a situation that is beyond fixing.

The best lessons come from experience. Take notes when you first start out, as this is a great way to record successes and failures for future growing efforts. Regardless, never let yourself become discouraged.

Salt buildup on growing media.

Seeding Problems

Starting from seed has its pros and cons. Obviously, growing from seed means you have countless options to choose from when deciding what you want to grow. Time of year will not matter either, if you have the proper setup for heat and lighting.

FAILURE TO GERMINATE

There are several reasons seeds may not germinate. Sometimes it is just a matter of patience since some seeds take much longer to push through the soil than others. Here are some other possible factors that may affect germination.

TEMPERATURE: May be too high or too low. Most seeds prefer between 70° and 80° F (20–25° C) in order to germinate. Temperature is important, as this is the signal to seedlings that spring has arrived. We can create this environment by supplying a heating mat in areas that are too cool. Often, grow lights will provide heat as well, from above.

Other seeds like cooler conditions. Hard seed coats, such as those of beets and chard, do well in cooler temperatures. Check the seed package for special instructions, or search the internet to get proper growing instructions for the plant you're trying to grow.

SEEDS PLANTED TOO DEEP: As discussed in the previous chapter, it's important not to plant too deeply. Some seeds need light to germinate or require it as soon as the embryo breaks the seed coat. In most cases, small seeds only need to be shaken onto the soil surface and then lightly pressed down to ensure good contact. For larger seeds, going down a depth equal to twice its circumference is usually sufficient.

WATERING WOES: Seeds may not germinate if the soil is allowed to dry out or the soil is too wet. Improper watering is one of the biggest culprits. Once the irreversible process of germination begins, if the soil dries out, the swelling seed coat will dry out and the embryo that is trying to emerge

If the planting medium becomes too dry, it can impede germination.

is halted. If the soil is too wet, the chance of fungal infection increases. Try to keep the soil moisture so that the texture and feel is like that of a wrung-out, damp sponge—just barely moist to the touch.

LIGHT: Too much light or not enough darkness can also affect a seed's germination. Not all seeds need light to sprout, but all seedlings need it to grow. Read the instructions on the seed packet for any special lighting requirements.

WRONG SOIL MIX: Seeds like a nice, airy soil. Peat (or coconut coir) with some perlite is usually the choice of most growers, since it retains water, allows for air, and makes it possible for roots to easily navigate through the loose medium. Always

Plants, including sprouts and seedlings, are always seeking the light and will bend toward it.

use a sterile potting mix when starting seeds. Outdoor garden soil can harbor all sorts of pests and disease that can attack young seedlings. Peat or coir pellets are very easy to use and are ideal for the beginner.

SEEDS ARE TOO OLD: Seeds usually have an expiration date on the package. Some seeds will last for years, but others begin to lose their germination rate after just one year. If you are using seeds from a previous season, do a test run first to test their viability. Sprinkle a few seeds onto a wet paper towel and place them somewhere moderately warm, like on top of the refrigerator.

If after the suggested period of germination, fewer than half the seeds break dormancy, this batch of seeds is not worth growing. Of course, you can still plant them, but be prepared for a low germination rate. It is better to start with fresh seeds if you have a batch of seeds that are past their expiration date.

Seedling Troubles

A favorite sight for a gardener is to see the first signs of growth after seeding. However, excitement can quickly turn to frustration when the emerging seedlings begin to show signs of trouble. Here are some common problems that can occur.

SEEDLINGS TOPPLING OVER: Damping off disease is a common problem that attacks young seedlings right at the soil level, causing them to appear pinched at the stem. It will begin to brown and topple over.

SEEDLINGS ARE TALL AND LEGGY: Young seedlings will struggle if there is not enough light. They are stretching to reach the light source. Bring the plants up closer to the light source by propping a box under them. If that is not possible, then lower the light source down from above. As seedlings begin to grow, keep moving the light source up and away from the seedlings.

SEEDLINGS ARE BENT IN ONE DIRECTION: Again, this is a lighting issue—they are turning toward the light, a common behavior when the seedlings are placed on a window ledge. Rotate the trays or containers daily to prevent this problem.

DRY, CURLED LEAVES: Grow lights can be quite warm, and the air in our homes can be dry. It is possible that your seedlings are not getting enough moisture, so be sure to keep the soil consistently moist when they are just beginning to grow.

LEAVES AND STEMS ARE DROOPY: Roots need air. If the soil mix is kept too soggy, then the plant roots cannot breathe. It is easy to overwater small plants, since they cannot take up excessive moisture in the soil fast enough for it to dry out. Instead of overhead watering, try adding water to the tray so that the plants can soak up what they need without becoming waterlogged.

BROWN LEAF TIPS: Warm temperatures or lack of watering can cause this. Using a fan to help circulate the air will help if the problem is too much heat. If you don't have a heat issue, then this could be a sign of underwatering, which causes the plant to dry out beyond wilt point. Lastly, brown leaf tips could be the result of fertilizer burn. It's important to use a very weak fertilizer solution when starting a feeding program, increasing the fertilizer concentration as the plants grow and become vigorous.

Burned tips can result from a few issues: heat from the light source, underwatering, or fertilizer burn.

YELLOWING LEAVES AND HALTED GROWTH: The seed contains everything the plant needs to get started, but once the second set of leaves develops, it's time to feed your plants. Yellow leaves and slow growth can be signs of nitrogen deficiency, and this means it is time to start a weak solution designed for the vegetables you're growing.

BOTTOM TWO LEAVES ARE YELLOW/DYING: The first two leaves are the cotyledons, and once the plant has established itself with its third or fourth sets of leaves, the early leaves will begin to wither, yellow, and die. They have done their job of assisting the young plant in its first few stages of growth, and now the true leaves will take over. In other words, it is not a problem at all, but a natural event when the first two leaves die and fall off.

LEAVES APPEAR PURPLISH/REDDISH: If this symptom is also followed by stalled growth, you may have a phosphorus deficiency. If you are already using a fertilizer that is designed for vegetables, it may not be the food but the pH, since this affects the plant's ability to take up this nutrient. Check the soil with a pH test. If the pH comes back higher or lower than what the plant that you are growing requires, you may need to adjust it.

Growing in pots indoors requires different treatments than growing in an outdoor garden bed. Compost and other amendments work great outdoors for solving many issues, but they are not easily used in plants grown indoors in pots. For indoor plants, the solution is to adjust nutrient levels in the water.

The pH level is easy to determine with a pH tester like this one or pH plant sticks.

Adjusting pH in Potted Plants

TO RAISE PH IF THE POTTING MIX IS TOO ACIDIC: Add 1 teaspoon of lime (calcium carbonate) to a gallon of water and pour onto soil to completely moisten it. Check in a couple of weeks and repeat if necessary. Wash any splashed water off leaves immediately, as the solution can burn leaves if allowed to dry.

TO LOWER PH IF THE POTTING MIX IS TOO ALKALINE: Sulfur is available as granules and can be worked into the soil or mixed with water. Usually ½ teaspoon for a 6-inch pot is enough. Check and adjust in a couple of weeks if necessary.

Common Indoor Pests and Diseases

All gardeners will face pests or diseases at some point in their growing endeavors. Most are fairly common and even predictable when growing indoors. Learning how to identify these problems is the key to treatment and as your experience grows, how to avoid them all together.

GREEN ALGAE ON SOIL: This is common in peat- or coir-based soil mixes. The green algae won't harm the seedlings, but it can lead to other problems such as retaining too much moisture. Not only can this cause an overwatering situation, but fungus gnats love this environment and can quickly establish themselves in the spongy green layer. Using a small tool, you can easily scrape this off or break it up.

Taking care of thousands of vegetables and annuals every year has taught me that this annoying green soil topper needs to be taken care of the minute it's spotted. I have my staff groom the pots by simply turning them on their sides and using their fingers to scrape the surface off into a bin.

Besides the immediate aesthetics of cleaning up the plants, this practice allows the soil to properly dry out between waterings. The appearance of the green algae sometimes darkens the soil mix, making it look like it's wet when it is not—which can lead you to under-water the plants. It's best to remove this green algae immediately once it appears.

BOTRYTIS: This is a gray fuzzy mold that develops on leaves and stems and will spread easily if not addressed. The appearance of this mold is usually a result of decaying leaves, so it is important to remove any debris that falls down onto the soil. High humidity and bad circulation are two things that contribute to the development of this fungal problem. Use a small fan to help move the air around plants if humidity is an issue, and stay on top of grooming practices.

POWDERY MILDEW: This appears as gray spots or a fine, powdery layer of gray on leaves. Usually resulting from high humidity, powdery mildew can be prevented with good air circulation as well.

FUNGUS GNATS: While these tiny black flies are more of a nuisance than a danger to the plants, they can lay eggs in the soil, and the hatching larvae can attack the roots of plants. This is a result of overwatering, since fungus gnats love wet soil. Remove the top layer of soil and allow the plant to dry out. Replace the top with sand if the problem is severe—sand dries out quickly and prevents females from laying eggs.

Use yellow sticky traps as a nontoxic method of killing these pests. Adult gnats are attracted to yellow and will stick to the tape. It could take several weeks of this treatment to stop the cycle, but it should clear up if you are persistent.

Natural controls like yellow sticky paper can greatly reduce fungus gnat problems.

APHIDS: These sap suckers usually appear as small green or black insects along stems and leaves of young shoots. Remove the stems that are heavily attacked, and use a few drops of dish soap mixed in water to spray directly onto the pests.

THRIPS: Thrips usually appear to be small papery brown spots on leaves. Quite often, thrips attack tomatoes, squash, and beans in a greenhouse environment. They scrape at the leaves and fruit and suck the juices from the plant. If you rustle the plant, these pests will fly up and then return back to the plant. Use a soap and water solution to control, spraying the undersides of the leaves.

SPIDER MITES: Spider mites first appear as light dots on leaves, which then may dry up and fall off. Spider mites live on the underside of leaves in colonies and are very tiny. A spray mist of water can reveal the webbing they create. Remove as much of the infestation as possible, and use a soap and water solution to control them.

MEALYBUGS: Mealybugs appear as cottony masses in the creases or on the undersides of leaves. Look down into the junction where the stem meets the leaf if you suspect a problem. Signs are yellowing, curling leaves and a sticky residue. The pests feed on the plant's sugars and excrete them, leading to the growth of sooty molds. A soapy water solution helps to control them, or you can use a cotton swab dabbed with rubbing alcohol in affected areas.

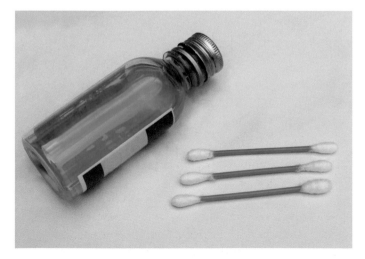

Isopropyl alcohol treats mealybugs. Spray on the affected area or use a cotton swab. *Shutterstock*

Hydroponic Growing Troubles

Growing hydroponically comes with its own set of possible troubles, which can be a little harder to pinpoint when you first get started with this form of gardening. There are four main problems associated with hydroponics:

- **Nutrition**

- **Pests**

- **Pathogens**

- **Growing environment**

Plants that are grown soilless still need air for their roots, and high humidity can cause fungal problems for leaves and stems. Proper air circulation above and below is as important as lighting and feeding.

SEEDLINGS WEAK IN ROCKWOOL CUBES: I had this problem and believe it was a pH issue. Rockwool cubes need to be rinsed several times and treated with a pH adjuster. Also, rockwool can hold a lot of moisture, so allow them to dry out slightly between waterings while the seedling is putting on roots.

STUNTED OR SLOW GROWTH: Temperature may be too cold. Ideally, the water solution should be between 60 and 90° F (15–20° C), with 80° F as optimal. Does the temperature drop at night by 10 degrees in the room when the lights go out? Extreme temperature fluctuations will have an effect on the liquid solution and how the plants react.

ROTTING STEMS AND LEAVES: When this occurs, humidity levels are likely too high. Provide proper air circulation and place a small fan near the growing device.

SALT BUILDUP: Salts can accumulate in the form of white crystals on the growing medium. If this

Salts can build on growing media and pots quickly.

occurs, flush the growing medium with a special flushing solution or a weak nutrient solution.

ALGAE BUILDUP IN SOLUTION: It's important that the solution chamber is completely blacked out, since light can encourage algae growth. This slimy growth can appear as green, brown, or black clinging to the walls and channels of the device. It can coat the root system and block up the pump and tubes, as well as deprive the water of oxygen available to plants. Flushing the system once every two weeks will help control this problem.

ODOR COMING FROM UNIT: Stagnation of the solution from lack of air flow can quickly result in unpleasant odors. Flush and clean the unit once every 2 weeks.

BROWN OR ROTTING ROOTS: Healthy roots are white and robust, while suffering roots become brown and slimy. This can be from a lack of oxygen, a nutrient deficiency, or an attack from a pathogen. Fungal, viral, and bacterial pathogens can be introduced into the solution from insects (fungus gnats), dust, or improperly sanitized equipment. If a plant is spotted with diseased roots, discard it and replace the nutrient solution.

NUTRIENT DEFICIENCY

Nutrient deficiency can be hard to identify, since most nutrients used are designed and balanced for proper uptake by plants. However, as previously discussed, many factors can affect how a plant absorbs nutrients. Temperature, pH, and electrical conductivity (EC) can affect nutrient availability.

PH: As previously discussed in Chapter 2, pH can affect what nutrients are available to plants.

TEMPERATURE: A temperature that is too cold or too warm may prevent the plants from effectively absorbing necessary nutrients.

EC: This is the measurement of dissolved solids in the solution—which effectively means the strength of the liquid fertilizer. As the plants take up water and fertilizers, this can change. For instance, if the temperature is warm, more water is taken up by the plants and transpired, leaving behind a stronger solution with a higher EC. Frequent fresh flushings will help control buildup.

In recirculating units, plants may take up nutrients very quickly, leading to the solution lacking one or more essential nutrients necessary for

If a plant seems to be suffering, check the roots. Remove plants that appear to be brown and rotten from the growing chamber. *Shutterstock*

continuous healthy plant growth. Potassium, iron, nitrogen, and calcium are commonly deficient in solutions if left too long in between changes.

CALCIUM DEFICIENCY: Tomatoes and peppers are particularly affected when there is a lack of calcium available, which can result in blossom end rot. Lettuce will appear to have tip burn.

IRON DEFICIENCY: Leaves begin to yellow in the tissue between the dark green veins of the plant.

POTASSIUM DEFICIENCY: This causes scorching and curling leaf tips, as well as loss of leaves.

NITROGEN DEFICIENCY: Symptoms of nitrogen deficiency include poor plant growth, and pale green or yellowing leaves.

Keep Calm and Garden On

Every garden has its challenges, regardless of size or situation. Indoor gardening doesn't mean you get a pass on dealing with pests and diseases; nor can you just feed it and forget it. However, it also shouldn't become something that is difficult or unpleasant to manage, either.

Choose the countertop gardening method that best suits your skill set and the amount of time you have available to dedicate to gardening each day or week. Growing your own food indoors is fun and easy to do, but it is not completely maintenance-free.

When someone asks me at the garden center to help them design a garden that is maintenance-free, I joke and tell them that they are at the wrong store. The concrete and stone landscape supply yard that sells materials for patios and paved surfaces has plenty of options that will fulfill that request. There is no such thing as a maintenance-free garden, not even on your countertop. Period.

Keeping a logbook is a great way of monitoring your growing endeavors. Tracking the progress from the day the seeds are sown to the time of harvest will become a valuable reference tool. Essentials are dates, varieties, costs, pests, plant failures, and materials used (mediums and fertilizers). Organize these into a journal and record daily or weekly.

Since we live in an electronic age, this can be done with a simple software program or phone app. You could also create a complex electronic spreadsheet or use an electronic shared document to design a chart that can be accessed and updated from any computer or electronic device. Evernote is a popular note-taking app that can help you easily organize and track your progress. Check the reference section of this book for some downloadable apps designed for smartphones and tablets that make recording your daily activities easier.

Recording data from your 'grows' is easy to do with a smartphone app.

Resources

All the products listed in the Countertop Devices section of this book are available online and can be shipped to you without ever shopping in a store. The items of equipment I used in my tests were shipped to me for review, and working with these brands was a pleasure. Not only were the manufacturers extremely excited about supplying samples, but I also found that each company's customer service was exceptional. Part of my testing included looking through their forums, about pages, and FAQs to test the customer experience, and in every case I was impressed.

Most of the items used in the DIY section were either on hand in my own kitchen or easily picked up from local housewares stores. If you cannot find a local supplier, most products can be easily ordered online.

AeroGardens come in different sizes and colors. *Photo courtesy of AeroGarden*

Product Links

Below are links for some specific products, plus a few more suggestions I found along the way.

AEROGARDEN

Hydroponic gardening with just a touch of a finger! With the extensive line of units this company has to offer, you are certain to find an AeroGarden that works for you. I loved the ease of use, the digital tracker and schedule reminders, as well as the sleek look of the units themselves. Plus, they have an entire selection of grow pods designed to work with the units, helping you take the guesswork out of choosing the right varieties.

AEROGARDEN HARVEST UNIT: www.aerogarden.com/aerogardens/miracle-gro-aerogarden-harvest-premium-eggplant-1.html

POD SEED KITS: www.aerogarden.com/seed-kits/6-pod-seed-kits.html

See pages 103 and 105.

BACK TO THE ROOTS

I loved working with this company. They have a so many garden goodies and cool products that it was hard not to want them all. Their customer service is exceptional, and they respond to every query on their website. The ones featured in the book:

WATER GARDEN 2.0: https://backtotheroots.com/products/watergarden

MUSHROOM FARM: https://backtotheroots.com/products/mushroomfarm

SELF-WATERING TOMATO PLANTER: https://backtotheroots.com/products/self-watering-planter

See pages 108, 90, and 134, respectively.

ELHO

This is a family-owned company that has been creating beautiful pots and accessories for more than 50 years. Their products are innovative, modern, and designed to complement the home garden. The quality of the samples they sent was so high that I will be using them for many years to come.

ALL-IN-ONE GROW KIT: www.elho.com/287845/collection/our-collection/green-basics/green-basics-allin1-growkit.html

ALL-IN-ONE BRUSSELS HERB PLANTER: www.elho.com/401118/collection/our-collection/indoor/brussels/brussels-herbs-all-in-1.html

See page 99 for All-in-One Grow Kit.

HYDROFARM

In addition to having some hydroponic kits ready to go right out of the box, this company offers everything you need to build your own. From lighting to pumps and fertilizer, their selection of products is vast. They include videos and lots of product information that will help you decide what materials are required to grow successfully.

MEGAGARDEN SYSTEM: www.hydrofarm.com/p/MGSYS

SALAD BOX: https://hydrofarm.com/p/GCSB

See pages 105–106 for the MegaGarden system and page 101 for the Salad Box.

MODERN SPROUT

This company was launched in May 2013 with a successful Kickstarter campaign. The couple who designs these products really understands what an urban gardener needs to grow their own food. The products they design not only fit busy lifestyles, but they fit beautifully with your décor, as well.

GARDEN JAR THREE PACK: www.modsprout.com/collections/herb-kits/products/garden-jar-three-pack-italian

GROWHOUSE: www.modsprout.com/collections/grow-lights/products/growhouse

HYDRO PLANTER: www.modsprout.com/collections/hydro-planters/products/plug-in-planter-chalkboard

See pages 88, 83, and 102, respectively.

POTTING SHED CREATIONS

The products from this company are made in the U.S. and their philosophy ("people make better products than machines") says everything about their culture. Be warned: you are going to love everything on their website!

GROW BOTTLE: www.pottingshedcreations.com/grow-bottle-basil

MICRO GREENS WINDOWSILL KIT: www.pottingshedcreations.com/micro-greens-veggie

GARDEN-IN-A-BAG: http://www.pottingshedcreations.com/garden-in-a-bag-basil

See pages 86, 95, and 89, respectively.

SUNBLASTER LIGHTING

When I had the chance to chat with Russ at SunBlaster Horticultural Lighting, the conversation could have gone on for hours. His enthusiasm and passion for the products they create is clearly motivated by encouraging people to get growing. While they don't sell directly to the consumer from their website, they can provide links to the companies that do. Check out their incredible line of lighting essentials at SunBlaster: www.sunblasterlighting.com

See pages 96–98.

Information Resources

Here are some places to turn if you need further information.

FINDOOR GARDEN DEPOT: This website has some pretty technical articles, but if you're serious about growing indoors, you will appreciate the depth of knowledge found here. How-to videos and even feeding schedules can be found on this website. https://indoorgardendepot.com/index.php

MAXIMUM YIELD: An amazing source of information on hydroponic growing. Dr. Lynette Morgan is an expert in hydroponics, and her contributing articles provide a wealth of information. www.maximumyield.com

PROMIX: I have had the pleasure of working with this company for many years, as they supply the soil mixes and mycorrhizae fertilizers for many of the projects on my website. They are committed to quality and offer a range of soil mixes that suit any growing situation. The training center on their website also has lots of information on growing mediums. www.pthorticulture.com/en/training-center

SIMPLY HYDROPONICS AND ORGANICS: In addition to offering organic fertilizers, books, and hydroponic supplies, they also offer online courses that will help you become an expert in no time. An extensive article and reference section that will answer all your questions. www.simplyhydro.com

Helpful Gardening Apps

These apps make recordkeeping so much easier.

EPLANT: This is a gardening journal app with access to Wikispecies and Wikipedia for detailed information about the plants you grow. Everything can be documented, from price to care for your indoor gardening. There are some costs associated with this app. Available at iTunes.

GARDENING COMPANION: This app has a ton of features, from setting reminders and journaling your garden activities to a wealth of online gardening information and troubleshooting tips. Available in the iTunes store.

GROLOG: This is a perfect app for growers to help them track their progress and monitor their gardens. It creates reports and logs data for everything from nutrient solutions to light settings. This is an app for the serious grower. Available at Google Play Store and iTunes.

GROW JOURNAL: This is a basic, simple app without a lot of extra information. It's designed to allow you to record information about the plants you are growing, track progress, and set reminders. If you are looking for an app without all the bells and whistles, this is a good one to try out. Available at Google Play Store.

Other Helpful Online Sources

And I'd be remiss not to mention these.

MOTHER EARTH NEWS: During online searches, I come to this website often. This online sustainable lifestyle magazine is packed with helpful articles, DIY projects, and information on growing organically. www.motherearthnews.com

SOW AND DIPITY: This is my personal website, where I share garden crafts, recipes, and fun DIYs to inspire folks to get growing. Many of the projects in this book are discussed beyond the initial setup, so if you wish to see the ongoing progress in more detail, be sure to visit: www.sowanddipity.com

INDEX

About the Author

Shelley Levis is a passionate horticulturist, speaker, writer, and garden designer. She is an editor and content creator for *Urbanique* magazine, a regular contributor to a variety of newspapers and magazines, and the voice behind the popular gardening blog "Sow & Dipity." Her creative DIY garden projects have been featured in the *Huffington Post*, *Fine Gardening* and *GreenCraft* magazines, and other publications.